Baking
with kids

Baking
with kids

LINDA COLLISTER
photography by Polly Wreford

RYLAND
PETERS
& SMALL

LONDON NEW YORK

Senior Designer Megan Smith
Commissioning Editor Julia Charles
Production Gemma Moules
Art Director Anne-Marie Bulat
Publishing Director Alison Starling

Food Stylist Joss Herd
Stylist Helen Trent
Indexer Hilary Bird

First published in the United States in 2006
by Ryland Peters & Small, Inc.
519 Broadway, 5th Floor
New York, NY 10012
www.rylandpeters.com
10 9 8 7 6 5 4 3 2

Text © Linda Collister 2006
Design and photographs
© Ryland Peters & Small 2006

Notes

All spoon measurements are level unless
otherwise specified. Ovens should be preheated
to the specified temperatures. All ovens work
slightly differently. I recommend using an oven
thermometer and suggest you consult the maker's
handbook for any special instructions—particularly
if you are using a fan-assisted oven as you may
need to adjust cooking temperatures.

Author's acknowledgments
I would like to thank the following for their help
with this book: Barbara Levy, Julia Charles, Megan
Smith, Gemma Moules, Polly Wreford, Joss Herd,
Helen Trent, Dan, Stevie, Emily Hertz, and last but
not least, all of the delightful children featured in
the photographs.

**Library of Congress
Cataloging-in-Publication Data**

Collister, Linda.
   Baking with kids / Linda Collister ; photography
by Polly Wreford.
     p. cm.
   Includes index.
   ISBN-13: 978-1-84597-220-2
   ISBN-10: 1-84597-220-1
   1. Baking--Juvenile literature.   I. Title.
TX765.C6125 2006
641.8'15--dc22

                         2006012203

Printed in China.

*To Elsa Petersen-Schepelern
(1948–2005) who was
responsible for the birth of
this book.*

contents

introduction

Baking is irresistible to any child: you turn a bag of flour, a carton of eggs, a heap of sugar, and a couple of sticks of butter into a cake! Call it magic, chemistry, or just a chance to lick the frosting bowl—it's great fun. Cooking and eating together is a delightful part of family life and a vital part of a child's education. It's a fun way to learn—not just about food and nutrition, but also about planning, co-operation, organization, and patience.

So, at what age should you get the kids involved? Our children started by mixing bowls of pancake batter at 18 months. They came with us to farmers' markets and to fishmongers' and butchers' shops and helped to plan and shop for meals. Two-year-olds love playing with a piece of dough. At three they can be making cookies, shaping bread rolls, and decorating cupcakes. Our children are older now, but

they still like playing with dough; if it is too wet for soccer after school, they bring their friends in to make fresh pasta noodles!

Each of my children still picks the dinner menu one night a week and helps with preparation. We grow tomatoes, strawberries, plums, and herbs in tubs on our patio garden. The children feel a great sense of achievement when eating what they have produced. We talk about how good fruit and vegetables taste, about the difference in flavor between apple varieties, about which of our tomatoes works best in a simple salad, and about how important they are for our health.

In the kitchen you need some ground rules so that your children quickly get into a habit of hygiene and safety. Wash hands, pull up long sleeves, avoid dangly jewelry and fussy clothes, tie back long hair, and wear an apron. They may be common

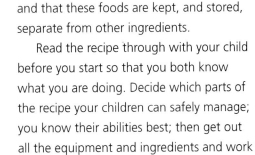

sense, but explaining the reasons behind the rules helps! Make sure children realize that kitchen knives and other equipment are not toys and must be treated carefully. Tell them that the oven can get very hot, so they should keep their distance, and explain why cutting boards, kitchen counters, and dish towels must be kept very clean. It's most important that everyone washes their hands and any cutting boards and knives really well with plenty of soap and hot water after handling raw chicken or meat, and that these foods are kept, and stored, separate from other ingredients.

Read the recipe through with your child before you start so that you both know what you are doing. Decide which parts of the recipe your children can safely manage; you know their abilities best; then get out all the equipment and ingredients and work together. If possible, invest in a few pieces of good-quality, child-friendly equipment such as nonstick baking sheets, a roasting pan, bowls with nonslip rubber bases, a rotary whisk, some short-handled wooden spoons, a bowl scraper, a safe cheese grater, a kitchen timer, and oven mitts. Older children with cooking experience can usually take a cake out of the oven without assistance, but straining a pan full of boiling pasta is always best done by an adult. NEVER leave a child under 10 alone in the kitchen to cook or use the microwave without adult supervision.

Accept that there will be a lot of clearing up, but give each child a specific task, such as sweeping the floor, rather than a long list of duties. Why not put on one of their favorite CDs!

Cooking is fun, brings a huge sense of achievement, and—of course—something wonderful to eat. Happy baking!

teatime favorites

Apple crumble is one of our favorite family desserts. We came up with this tasty muffin so that we could enjoy the lovely, crumbly topping and fresh appley taste at teatime as well as after dinner. You could also pop one in your school lunchbox.

apple crumble muffins

Makes 12 muffins

For the topping:
4 tablespoons unsalted butter, chilled
¼ cup coarse brown or superfine sugar
⅓ cup all-purpose flour
½ cup sliced almonds, ground (optional)

For the base:
2 cups all-purpose flour
2 teaspoons baking powder
⅞ cup superfine or granulated sugar
1 unwaxed lemon
10 tablespoons unsalted butter
2 extra-large eggs
½ cup whole milk
2 medium apples, washed

a 12-hole muffin pan lined with paper muffin cases

1 ASK AN ADULT TO HELP YOU preheat the oven to 375°F.

2 Make the topping first. Cut the butter into small pieces and put it into a mixing bowl with the sugar, flour, and ground almonds. Rub the ingredients together until they look like small peas. Put on one side until needed.

3 Set a large strainer over a mixing bowl. Tip the flour into the strainer. Measure the baking powder into the strainer then sift into the bowl. Add the sugar to the bowl and mix in with a wooden spoon.

4 Carefully grate the yellow zest from the lemon (or use a special citrus zester) leaving the white pith on the fruit. Add to the bowl and stir in. Make a well in the center of the ingredients.

5 ASK AN ADULT TO HELP YOU carefully melt the butter in a small pan over low heat, or you can melt it in the microwave. Pour into the well.

6 Break the eggs into a small bowl. Pick out any pieces of shell, then beat the eggs with a fork until the yolks are just broken up. Tip into the well in the mixing bowl then pour in the milk. Mix gently with a wooden spoon.

7 Spoon the mixture into the paper muffin cases, making sure there is the same amount in each.

8 Carefully cut each apple into quarters, then cut out the core. Roughly chop the apples. Scatter the apple pieces on top of the muffin mixture. Sprinkle the topping over the apples.

9 ASK AN ADULT TO HELP YOU put the muffins in the preheated oven to bake for 30 minutes, until golden brown. ASK AN ADULT TO HELP YOU carefully remove the pan from the oven and leave to cool for 2 minutes. Transfer the muffins to a wire rack and leave to cool completely. Store your muffins in an airtight container and eat them within 3 days.

Scones are a traditional teatime treat. They are a cross between bread and cake. Eat them cut in two and spread with butter and jam or some honey. A traditional British "cream tea" in a teashop is scones spread with strawberry jam and heavy "clotted" cream. You can flavor your scones with sultanas if you like, or leave out the sugar and add some grated cheese with a big pinch of cayenne pepper.

scones

Makes about 8 scones

Basic recipe:
2 cups all-purpose flour
4 teaspoons baking powder
a pinch of salt
¼ cup superfine or granulated sugar
4 tablespoons unsalted butter, at room temperature
1 extra-large egg
about ½ cup whole or half-fat milk

a nonstick baking sheet
a round cookie cutter, about 2½ inches diameter

1 ASK AN ADULT TO HELP YOU preheat the oven to 425°F. Put a little butter on a piece of paper towel and rub it over the baking sheet to lightly grease it.

2 Set a strainer over a mixing bowl. Tip the flour, baking powder, salt, and sugar in it and sift into the bowl. Using an ordinary round-bladed table knife, cut up the butter into tiny pieces and add to the bowl.

3 Toss the pieces of butter in the flour so they are well coated, then rub the butter into the flour—to do this, pick up a handful of the mixture with your fingers, then rub the mixture between the very ends of your fingers so the bits of butter become smaller and smaller as they mix with the flour. Keep rubbing in until the whole mixture looks like crumbs. Make a hollow in the centre of the crumby mixture.

4 Break the egg into a measuring pitcher. Mix with a fork just to break up the yolk and the white then pour in enough milk to make up the mixture to ⅔ cup.

5 Pour three-quarters of the milk mixture into the hollow. Using the table knife, stir the liquid and the flour mixture together to make a soft, coarse-looking dough. If the dough is dry and crumbly and won't stick together, stir in more of the milk mixture a tablespoon at a time.

6 Tip out the dough onto a kitchen counter lightly covered with flour. Work and knead the ball of dough with your hands for a few seconds so it looks smoother. Dip your hands in a little more flour then pat out the dough until it is about 1¼ inches thick. Dip the cutter in flour then cut out rounds. Gather up the scraps into a ball, then press out and cut out more rounds.

7 Put all the rounds onto the prepared baking sheet, setting them slightly apart. ASK AN ADULT TO HELP YOU put the sheet in the preheated oven to bake for 12–15 minutes, until golden brown. ASK AN ADULT TO HELP YOU remove the sheet from the oven and set it on a heatproof counter. Transfer the scones to a wire rack using a metal spatula or fish slice. Your scones are best eaten the same day and are also good toasted.

This is a really quick and easy recipe. The buns are packed with a mixture of dried fruit—cherries, cranberries, strawberries, and blueberries. You'll find bags of these mixed dried "berries and cherries" in grocery stores, or you can also use jumbo raisins. Why not experiment and make up your own combination?

cherry berry buns

Makes 18 small buns

2 cups all-purpose flour
4 teaspoons baking powder
¼ teaspoon apple-pie spice
7 tablespoons unsalted butter,
   at room temperature
⅓ cup soft light brown sugar
¾–1 cup cherry berry mix
   (see above)
1 extra-large egg
5–6 tablespoons milk
granulated or coarse brown
   sugar, for sprinkling

*2 nonstick baking sheets,
   lightly greased*

1 ASK AN ADULT TO HELP YOU preheat the oven to 400°F.

2 Set a large strainer over a mixing bowl. Tip the flour into the strainer. Add the baking powder and apple-pie spice to the strainer and sift these ingredients into the bowl.

3 Cut the butter into small pieces and add to the bowl. Work the butter into the flour by rubbing it in with the tips of your fingers—to do this pick up some of the mixture with just the ends of your fingers and thumb, then rub your fingers and thumb together so the butter pieces get smaller and smaller and gradually disappear so that the mixture looks like bread crumbs.

4 Stir in the soft light brown sugar and cherry berry mix and make a well in the mixture.

5 Break the egg into a small bowl. Pick out any pieces of shell, then add 4 tablespoons of milk and beat the mixture with a fork just to break up the egg and combine it with the milk.

6 Pour the milk and egg into the well in the flour mixture. Mix all the ingredients together with a round-bladed knife to make a firm dough. If there are dry crumbs or the dough won't mix together, add another tablespoon of milk.

7 Drop spoonfuls of the mixture on to the prepared sheets, using about a heaped tablespoon of mixture for each bun, spacing them slightly apart. Sprinkle each bun with a little sugar.

8 ASK AN ADULT TO HELP YOU put the buns in the preheated oven to bake for 15 minutes, until golden brown. ASK AN ADULT TO HELP YOU remove the sheets from the oven and leave to cool for 2 minutes. Transfer the buns to a wire rack to cool completely. Store your buns in an airtight container and eat them within 3 days.

Here is something you can do on a rainy day. Bake some cupcakes and decorate them with a fudgy topping and some jelly beans or anything you like—try chocolate chips, jimmies, or colored sprinkles.

chocolate cupcakes

Makes 12 cupcakes

For the cakes:
1⅓ cups all-purpose flour
1 teaspoon baking powder
a pinch of salt
¼ cup unsweetened cocoa
¾ cup superfine or granulated
   sugar
7 tablespoons unsalted butter,
   very soft
2 extra-large eggs
½ cup whole milk

For the frosting:
3½ oz. bittersweet chocolate
1 tablespoon golden syrup or
   light corn syrup
2 tablespoons unsalted butter

*a 12-hole muffin pan lined
   with paper muffin cases*

1 ASK AN ADULT TO HELP YOU preheat the oven to 350°F.

2 Place a large strainer over a mixing bowl. Tip the flour, baking powder, salt, cocoa, and sugar into the strainer as you measure them, then sift into the bowl.

3 Add the butter to the bowl. Break the eggs into a small bowl, pick out any pieces of shell then beat the eggs with a fork until they are a bit frothy.

4 Pour the eggs and milk into the larger bowl. Use a wooden spoon to mix all the ingredients together to make a smooth cake batter.

5 Carefully spoon the cake mixture into the paper cases, putting an equal amount into each one.

6 ASK AN ADULT TO HELP YOU put the cakes in the preheated oven to bake for 20 minutes, until just firm to the touch. ASK AN ADULT TO HELP YOU remove the pan from the oven and leave to cool for about 2 minutes. Transfer the cupcakes to a wire rack and leave to cool completely.

7 While the cakes are cooling, make the frosting. Break up the chocolate and put it in a small heatproof bowl with the golden syrup and butter. ASK AN ADULT TO HELP YOU place the bowl over a saucepan filled with steaming hot but not boiling water. Stir gently with a wooden spoon until smooth and melted. Remove the bowl from the pan. Leave to cool for 5 minutes.

8 To finish the cakes, spoon the smooth runny chocolate frosting on top of the cakes and add your decoration. Leave it to set before eating. Store your cupcakes in an airtight container and eat them within 4 days.

These lovely chewy bars are made with a basic mixture of butter, honey, sugar, oats, flour, and baking powder. You can add your own favorite dried fruits, seeds, and nuts or you could replace the nuts with chopped dates, dried figs, or dried cranberries. Use my recipe below as a starting point and experiment to find out what you like best to create your own special version.

granola bars

Makes 16 bars

7 tablespoons unsalted butter

⅓ cup clear honey

2 tablespoons soft light
   brown sugar

3½ cups rolled oats

2 tablespoons all-purpose
   flour

½ teaspoon baking powder

⅓ cup soft dried apricots,
   chopped

2 tablespoons sunflower
   seeds

2 tablespoons sesame seeds

2 tablespoons raisins

3¼ oz. mixed nuts or dried
   fruit and nut mix, chopped

8 x 10 inch baking pan
nonstick baking parchment

1 ASK AN ADULT TO HELP YOU preheat the oven to 325°F. Grease the inside of the baking pan with a small amount of soft butter on a piece of paper towel. Cut a rectangle from a sheet of baking parchment the same size as the pan and fit it into the bottom of the pan.

2 Put the butter in a large saucepan. Add the honey and sugar. ASK AN ADULT TO HELP YOU put the saucepan over low heat. Heat gently until the butter melts. Carefully remove the pan from the heat. Stir gently with a wooden spoon. Tip all the rest of the ingredients into the pan and stir well with the wooden spoon.

3 Transfer the mixture to the prepared baking pan and spread evenly. Press the mixture into the pan with the back of a spoon.

4 ASK AN ADULT TO HELP YOU put the pan in the preheated oven to bake for 30 minutes, until golden brown. ASK AN ADULT TO HELP YOU remove the pan from the oven and put it on a wire rack. Leave it to cool completely.

5 Loosen the mixture from the pan by running a round-bladed knife inside the edge of the pan, then flip the pan upside down onto a cutting board so the granola mixture falls out in one piece. Cut it into 16 bars. Store your bars in an airtight container and eat them within a week.

This easy recipe makes crunchy cookies that are perfect to enjoy with a glass of milk when you get home from school. The ginger is what makes them spicy and the molasses gives them a lovely toffee flavor.

ginger snaps

Makes 24 cookies

2⅓ cups all-purpose flour
1 teaspoon bicarbonate
   of soda
3 teaspoons baking powder
3 teaspoons ground ginger
1 teaspoon ground cinnamon
1 cup superfine or granulated
   sugar, plus extra for
   sprinkling
1 stick unsalted butter
¼ cup molasses
1 extra-large egg

2 nonstick baking sheets

1 ASK AN ADULT TO HELP YOU preheat the oven to 325°F. Grease the baking sheets with soft butter, using a piece of paper towel.

2 Set a strainer over a large bowl. Tip the flour, bicarbonate of soda, baking powder, ground ginger, and cinnamon into the strainer and sift into the bowl. Add the sugar and mix in with a wooden spoon. Make a hollow in the middle of the flour mixture.

3 Put the butter and molasses in a small saucepan. ASK AN ADULT TO HELP YOU melt the butter and molasses gently over very low heat—warm the pan just enough to melt the ingredients, don't let the mixture become hot.

4 Carefully pour the melted mixture into the hollow in the flour.

5 Break the egg into a small bowl, remove any pieces of shell and break it up with a fork.

6 Pour the egg into the hollow on top of the melted mixture. Mix all the ingredients together with a wooden spoon. As soon as the dough starts to come together, put your hands into the bowl and start to push the warm dough together. If the dough feels a bit too warm, wait for it to cool.

7 When the dough has come together, use your hands to roll it into 24 balls, slightly smaller than table tennis balls, but larger than big marbles.

8 Arrange the balls well apart on the prepared baking sheets then flatten them with your fingers. Sprinkle them with a little sugar.

9 ASK AN ADULT TO HELP YOU put the cookies in the preheated oven to bake for about 15 minutes, until lightly browned around the edges.

10 ASK AN ADULT TO HELP YOU remove the sheets from the oven. Leave them on a heatproof counter to cool for 5 minutes. When the cookies feel firm enough to move, gently lift them on to a wire rack using a large metal spatula or fish slice. Let them cool completely. Store your cookies in an airtight container and eat them within 5 days.

holiday spice cookies

Makes about 24 cookies

2¼ cups all-purpose flour
2 teaspoons ground cinnamon
½ teaspoon ground ginger
½ teaspoon apple-pie spice
1½ sticks unsalted butter,
  straight from the fridge,
  plus extra butter for
  greasing
6 tablespoons clear honey
thin ribbon, thread, or raffia,
  to hang
writing frosting pens and
  silver balls, to decorate

*a selection of shaped cookie
  cutters such as stars,
  Christmas trees, angels,
  bells, and reindeer*
2 nonstick baking sheets

1 Lightly grease the baking sheets with soft butter, using a piece of paper towel.

2 Put the flour, cinnamon, ginger, and apple-pie spice in the bowl of a food processor. Using an ordinary table knife, cut the butter into small pieces and add to the bowl of the processor.

3 ASK AN ADULT TO HELP YOU run the processor until the mixture looks like fine crumbs.

4 Measure the honey into the bowl of the processor and WITH ADULT HELP run the processor until the mixture comes together to make a ball of dough.

5 ASK AN ADULT TO HELP YOU remove the blade from the bowl, then remove the dough from the bowl. Wrap the dough in plastic wrap or waxed paper and put it into the fridge until it is firm enough to roll out—about 30 minutes.

6 ASK AN ADULT TO HELP YOU preheat the oven to 350°F.

7 Sprinkle the kitchen counter and a rolling pin with flour. Gently roll out the dough until it is about ¼ inch thick. Cut out shapes using your cutters. Gather up the trimmings into a ball then roll out and cut more shapes. For decorations you can hang up, make a small hole at the top of each cookie with a toothpick (make sure the hole is large enough to thread a ribbon through).

8 Arrange the shapes slightly apart on the baking sheets. ASK AN ADULT TO HELP YOU put them in the oven to bake for about 10 minutes, or until golden. ASK AN ADULT TO HELP YOU carefully remove the trays from the oven. Put them on a heatproof counter and leave to cool for 5 minutes. Gently transfer the cookies to a wire rack and leave until cold.

9 Decorate however you like: thread them with ribbon then ice using colored frosting pens and silver balls. Leave until set then hang up. Eat your cookies as soon as possible or store them in an airtight container and eat within 5 days.

It's fun to make your own edible holiday
decorations or treats for a special birthday
party. You cut shapes out of cookie dough
and have lots of fun decorating them with
colored icing and silver balls.

If you love chocolate then this is the
cookie for you! These are quick and
easy to make and fun to share. If you
want a less sweet, crunchy chocolate
cookie, just replace the white chocolate
chips with walnut pieces.

triple choc cookies

Makes 24 cookies

9 tablespoons unsalted butter,
   at room temperature

½ cup superfine or granulated
   sugar

⅔ cup firm-packed light
   brown sugar

1 extra-large egg

1⅔ cups all-purpose flour

2½ tablespoons unsweetened
   cocoa

½ teaspoon baking powder

½ teaspoon baking soda

a pinch of salt

⅔ cup bittersweet chocolate
   chips

⅔ cup white chocolate chips

2–3 nonstick baking sheets,
   ungreased

1 ASK AN ADULT TO HELP YOU preheat the oven to 350°F.

2 Put the butter in a mixing bowl or the bowl of an electric mixer. Add both the sugars and beat with a wooden spoon or the whisk attachment until the mixture looks very soft and fluffy. Scrape down the sides of the bowl with a plastic spatula every now and then so all the ingredients get fully beaten.

3 Break the egg into a small bowl. Remove any pieces of shell then break up the egg with a fork. Add the egg to the mixing bowl and beat the mixture well.

4 Set a strainer over the mixing bowl. Tip the flour, cocoa, baking powder, baking soda, and salt into the strainer then sift these ingredients into the bowl. Mix in with the wooden spoon, or with the electric mixer on low speed.

5 Add all the chocolate chips to the bowl and mix in with a wooden spoon until everything is thoroughly combined.

6 To make the mixture into cookies, dip your hands in cold water so they are just damp then take a small amount of the mixture—about a rounded tablespoon—and roll it into a ball. Set the ball on to the prepared baking sheet, then make 23 more balls in the same way. Set the balls about 1½ inches apart on the sheets.

7 ASK AN ADULT TO HELP YOU put the cookies in the preheated oven to bake for 15 minutes. ASK AN ADULT TO HELP YOU carefully remove the sheets from the oven and leave to cool for 5 minutes before transferring the cookies to a wire rack. Leave to cool completely, then store in an airtight container. Eat your cookies within a week of baking them.

These irresistible cookies are made with the same oats that you eat for breakfast. Why not make a box for the next "bake sale" at school? You can add dried fruit like jumbo raisins or dried cherries and cranberries, chopped nuts, or even chocolate chips.

oatie cookies

Makes 18 cookies

9 tablespoons unsalted butter
½ cup superfine or granulated sugar
⅔ cup firm-packed soft dark brown sugar
1 extra-large egg
1½ cups rolled oats
scant 1 cup all-purpose flour
a pinch of salt
¼ teaspoon bicarbonate of soda
½ teaspoon vanilla extract
½ cup raisins, dried cherries, dried cranberries, chopped nuts, or chocolate chips

2 nonstick baking sheets

1 ASK AN ADULT TO HELP YOU preheat the oven to 350°F. Put a little soft butter on a piece of paper towel and rub it over the baking sheets to grease them.

2 Put the butter in a saucepan that's big enough to hold all the ingredients. ASK AN ADULT TO HELP YOU melt the butter over low heat. Remove the pan from the heat and put it on a heatproof counter. Tip both the sugars into the pan and mix into the butter with a wooden spoon. Make sure you stir until all the lumps of sugar have been broken up.

3 Break the egg into a small bowl. Pick out any pieces of shell and lightly beat the egg with a fork just to break it up. Pour the egg into the pan and mix it in.

4 Add the rolled oats to the pan and stir well. Add the flour, salt, bicarbonate of soda, and vanilla extract and mix well.

5 Finally add your choice of dried fruit, nuts, or chocolate and mix until thoroughly combined.

6 Using a rounded tablespoon of mixture for each cookie, drop the mixture onto the sheets making sure they are well apart. Gently flatten the mounds of dough with your fingers. ASK AN ADULT TO HELP YOU put the cookies in the preheated oven to bake for 13–15 minutes, until lightly browned. ASK AN ADULT TO HELP YOU remove the sheets from the oven. Leave to cool for 2 minutes then use a metal spatula to lift the cookies off the sheets and onto a wire rack to cool completely. Store your cookies in an airtight container and eat them within 5 days.

Popovers are a sort of puffy, muffin-sized roll with a crisp brown crust and a hollow, moist inside. The name is said to come from the fact that as the batter bakes it expands and "pops over" the sides of the cups in the baking pan. You can eat them straight from the oven with maple syrup or honey and a pat of butter. The batter takes seconds to make in a food processor so why not try them for breakfast at the weekend or as a delicious after-school snack?

popovers

Makes 12 popovers

1 cup whole or half-fat milk
1 cup all-purpose flour
¼ teaspoon salt
1 tablespoon wheatgerm or
oat bran
3 extra-large eggs
2 tablespoons melted butter

a 12-hole muffin pan or
flexible molds set on a
baking sheet

1 ASK AN ADULT TO HELP YOU preheat the oven to 425°F. Put a little butter on a piece of paper towel and rub it inside the holes of the muffin pan or molds so they are lightly greased.

2 Put the milk, flour, salt and wheatgerm or oat bran into the bowl of a food processor or blender.

3 Break the eggs into a small bowl, pick out any pieces of shell then pour the eggs into the processor or blender.

4 ASK AN ADULT TO HELP YOU melt the butter in a small pan over low heat, or in the microwave. Pour the melted butter into the processor or blender. Put the lid on tightly and WITH ADULT HELP run the processor or blender for about 20 seconds or until you have a smooth batter.

5 ASK AN ADULT TO HELP YOU remove the processor blade, then pour the batter into a jug. If you have a blender that pours you don't need to do this. Pour the batter into the 12 holes of the muffin pan or into the flexible molds, so that each one is about half full.

6 ASK AN ADULT TO HELP YOU put the popovers in the preheated oven to bake for 25 minutes. Then, without opening the oven door, turn down the heat to 350°F and bake for another 15 minutes. ASK AN ADULT TO HELP YOU remove the popovers from the oven and tip them out of the muffin pan or molds onto a serving plate. Eat your popovers straightaway while they are still warm from the oven.

This loaf makes a tasty teatime snack. Cut it into thick slices and either eat it plain or spread it with cream cheese or hazelnut and chocolate spread. It's even good toasted! You will need to use really ripe bananas.

banana loaf

Makes 1 medium loaf cake

2 cups all-purpose flour
1 teaspoon baking powder
a good pinch of salt
½ cup firm-packed soft light
  brown sugar
⅓ cup superfine of granulated
  sugar
7 tablespoons unsalted butter
2 extra-large eggs
9 oz. peeled ripe bananas—
  about 2 large bananas
½ cup bittersweet chocolate
  chips or chunks

a 2 lb. loaf pan
nonstick baking parchment

1 ASK AN ADULT TO HELP YOU preheat the oven to 350°F. Put a small amount of soft butter on a piece of paper towel and rub it around the inside of the pan so it lightly greased. Cut a strip of baking parchment the same width as the pan and as long as the base plus the height of each end of the pan. Fit the paper into the pan so it covers the base and the two short ends.

2 Put the flour, baking powder, and salt into a strainer set over a mixing bowl and sift into the bowl. Add the sugars and stir in with a wooden spoon. Make a well in the center.

3 Put the butter into a small pan. ASK AN ADULT TO HELP YOU melt the butter over very low heat or do it in the microwave. Break the eggs into a small bowl and pick out any pieces of shell. Beat the eggs with a fork just to break them up.

4 Add the melted butter and the eggs to the well in the flour mixture.

5 Put the bananas on to a plate and mash with a fork, but don't make them too smooth or like a purée—there should still be some lumpy bits.

6 Add the bananas and chocolate chips to the well in the bowl.

7 Mix all the ingredients together with the wooden spoon until thoroughly combined, with no streaks of flour visible.

8 Spoon the mixture into the prepared pan and spread evenly. ASK AN ADULT TO HELP YOU put the loaf in the preheated oven to bake for 55 minutes, until it's golden brown. To test if the loaf is cooked ASK AN ADULT TO HELP YOU carefully remove the loaf from the oven then push a toothpick or skewer into the center of it. If the stick comes out clean the loaf is cooked; if the stick is covered in sticky mixture then bake the loaf for another 5 minutes and test again.

9 ASK AN ADULT TO HELP YOU remove the pan from the oven and put it on a wire rack to cool completely, then remove the loaf from the pan and peel off the paper. Store your banana loaf in an airtight container and eat it within 5 days.

Other ideas
Add 1 cup walnut or pecan pieces to the mixture when you mix in the bananas. Or you could try ⅓ cup sultanas or chocolate chips.

big bakes

This is a really delicious and chocolatey cake, perfect for birthdays—just decorate it and add candles! It tastes best when it's made the day before the party.

chocolate fudge birthday cake

Makes 1 large cake that will give 8–10 slices

For the cake:
2 cups all-purpose flour
2 teaspoons baking powder
1 teaspoon baking soda
a pinch of salt
3½ oz. bittersweet chocolate
3 tablespoons unsweetened cocoa
½ cup water, very hot but not boiling
1½ sticks unsalted butter, softened
1¼ cups superfine or granulated sugar
3 extra-large eggs
1 cup plain yogurt (whole milk or low-fat NOT fat-free)

For the chocolate frosting:
½ cup heavy cream
2 oz. milk chocolate
2 oz. bittersweet chocolate
your choice of decorations

a springform cake pan, 9 inches diameter
nonstick baking parchment

1 ASK AN ADULT TO HELP YOU preheat the oven to 325°F.

2 Grease the inside of the cake pan with a little soft butter on a piece of paper towel. Cut a circle from a sheet of nonstick baking parchment —put the cake pan on the paper and draw around it. Using scissors, cut inside the line so you have a circle the same size as the pan. Fit this into the bottom of the pan.

3 Set a large strainer over a bowl and tip the flour, baking powder, baking soda, and salt into the strainer. Carefully sift these ingredients into the bowl. Put the bowl on one side until needed.

4 Break up the bittersweet chocolate and put it into a large heatproof mixing bowl. Mix in the cocoa. ASK AN ADULT TO HELP YOU pour on the very hot water. Leave for 1 minute then stir gently with a wooden spoon until the mixture is very smooth and melted. Put on one side.

5 Put the butter and sugar into the bowl of an electric mixer or a mixing bowl. Beat well with the whisk attachment or a wooden spoon.

6 Break the eggs into a small bowl, remove any pieces of shell, then gradually add the eggs to the bowl and beat really well until very smooth.

7 Pour the melted chocolate mixture into the bowl and mix well. Spoon in the yogurt and tip in the flour mixture and mix well.

8 Spoon the mixture into the prepared pan, then spread the mixture evenly so it is smooth.

9 ASK AN ADULT TO HELP YOU put the cake in the oven to bake for 55 minutes. To test if it is cooked ASK AN ADULT TO HELP YOU remove the cake from the oven and stick a toothpick into the middle, then carefully pull it out. The cake is cooked if the toothpick comes out clean; if the toothpick is sticky, bake for another 5 minutes then test again. ASK AN ADULT TO HELP YOU remove the cake from the oven and set the pan on a wire rack. Leave to cool for 5 minutes then loosen the cake by running a round-bladed knife inside the pan. Unclip the pan and leave the cake to cool completely. Don't worry if it sinks a bit.

10 To make the frosting, put the cream into a saucepan. ASK AN ADULT TO HELP YOU heat it until it is scalding hot, but not quite at a boil. Remove the pan from the heat. Break up the two kinds of chocolate and put it in a heatproof bowl. Carefully pour over the hot cream. Leave for about 2 minutes then stir until smooth. Leave to cool, the icing will thicken as it cools.

11 Set the cake upside down on a serving plate. Spread the frosting on the top and sides of the cake to cover it completely. Decorate with sprinkles and candy. Leave in a cool place until it is firm before you cut it. Store your cake in an airtight container and eat it within 5 days.

This is a very rich and moist cake with a hidden layer of golden marzipan. It's perfect for special occasions. Use a bag of mixed dried fruits like raisins and currants or try the "luxury" mix, which also includes chopped apricots and pineapple.

celebration cake

Makes 1 large cake

1⅔ cups all-purpose flour
2 teaspoons baking powder
½ cup less 1 tablespoon sliced
   almonds, ground
1½ sticks unsalted butter,
   very soft
1 cup firm-packed soft light
   brown sugar
4 extra-large eggs
2 tablespoons whole milk
2½ cups dried mixed fruit
¾ cup almond paste
2 tablespoons sliced or
   slivered almonds

a round deep cake pan or
   springform cake pan,
   8 inches diameter
nonstick baking parchment

1 ASK AN ADULT TO HELP YOU preheat the oven to 350°F.

2 Put a little butter on a piece of paper towel and rub it around the inside of the pan. Cut out a circle from a sheet of nonstick baking parchment—put the pan on the paper and draw around it. Cut inside the line so you have a circle that fits inside the pan. Fit the circle into the pan so it sticks to the base. Next cut a strip of baking parchment the circumference and depth of the pan and fit this inside so it sticks to the sides.

3 Put the flour, baking powder, ground almonds, butter, and sugar in a large mixing bowl. Break the eggs into the bowl then add the milk. Using a wooden spoon or an electric mixer (on slow speed) beat the mixture for 1 minute, or until it looks very smooth with no streaks.

4 Add the dried fruit to the bowl. Stir well with a wooden spoon until it looks evenly mixed.

5 Spoon half the cake mixture into the pan. Spread it evenly with the back of a spoon.

6 Using your hands, mold and press the almond paste into a round shape 7½ inches across. You can also roll out the almond paste with a rolling pin. Place it gently on top of the cake mix in the pan. Spoon the rest of the cake mix on top of the almond paste and spread it evenly. Sprinkle with the sliced almonds.

7 ASK AN ADULT TO HELP YOU put the cake in the preheated oven. Bake for 30 minutes then turn down the oven temperature to 325°F and bake for a further 1¼–1½ hours. To test if the cake is cooked, ASK AN ADULT TO HELP YOU remove it from the oven. Push a toothpick into the center of the cake, just down as far as the almond paste layer. If it comes out clean, the cake is ready; if it comes out sticky with cake mixture, cook for another 10 minutes.

8 When the cake is cooked, ASK AN ADULT TO HELP YOU remove it from the oven and stand the pan on a wire rack. Leave to cool completely, then turn the cake out of the pan and peel off the lining paper. Store your cake in an airtight container and eat it within a week.

yule log

Makes 1 large cake

For the sponge cake:
½ cup plus 1 tablespoons superfine sugar
4 extra-large eggs, at room temperature
½ teaspoon vanilla extract
3 tablespoons unsalted butter
1 cup all-purpose flour
½ teaspoon baking powder

For the filling and icing:
4–5 tablespoons chocolate hazelnut spread (Nutella)
½ cup heavy cream
3½ oz. bittersweet chocolate
confectioners' sugar, to sprinkle
your choice of decorations

a Swiss roll pan, 8 x 12 inches
2 sheets nonstick baking parchment

1 ASK AN ADULT TO HELP YOU preheat the oven to 400°F. Put a little soft butter on a piece of paper towel and rub it around the inside of the pan. Cut a rectangle of nonstick baking parchment to fit the pan—set the pan on the paper, draw around it, then cut just inside the line—and fit it into the pan to cover the base completely.

2 Put the sugar in a mixing bowl or the bowl of an electric mixer. Break the eggs into a small bowl, pick out any pieces of shell, then pour the eggs into the bowl with sugar. Add the vanilla extract. ASK AN ADULT TO HELP YOU melt the butter in a small saucepan over low heat, or in the microwave. Leave to cool until needed.

3 Using an electric whisk or the whisk attachment of the mixer ASK AN ADULT TO HELP YOU whisk the sugar and eggs together for 2 minutes or until very thick and foamy.

4 Set a strainer over the bowl. Tip the flour and baking powder into the strainer and sift it into the bowl. Gently fold into the egg mixture with a large metal spoon. Do this slowly and carefully so the air isn't knocked out of the mixture. Drizzle the melted butter over the top and fold it in quite quickly.

5 Pour the mixture into the prepared pan and spread it evenly using a plastic scraper or spatula. ASK AN ADULT TO HELP YOU put the sponge in the preheated oven to bake for 10 minutes. To test if the sponge is cooked ASK AN ADULT TO HELP YOU pull it out on the oven shelf and press the center lightly with a finger. If the cake is springy, it is cooked; if your finger leaves a dent, cook for 2 more minutes then test again.

6 ASK AN ADULT TO HELP YOU remove the cake from the oven. Leave for 1 minute to cool. Meanwhile, cover a wire rack with a dry paper towel, then a sheet of baking parchment. ASK AN ADULT TO HELP YOU carefully tip the sponge out onto the paper. Peel off the lining paper. Gently roll up the sponge with the other sheet of paper still inside. Leave the sponge on the wire rack until it is completely cold.

This is the cake the French make to celebrate Christmas, but its tradition goes back to the time of the pagan Vikings. They had a Yule log ceremony to celebrate the sun at the time of the winter solstice. Yule was Odin, the father of the gods, and a massive log of wood burned in his honor to bring luck. These days a small log is burned at a party on Christmas Eve and is always lit by a piece saved from last year.

The cake is a sponge roll, made by beating the eggs with an electric mixer or whisk, filled with ready-made chocolate spread, then covered with a rich chocolate cream. You can add decorations like robins, tiny trees, a cake candle, or a small sleigh filled with foil-wrapped candy or coins for presents.

7 Carefully unroll the sponge and discard the paper. Don't worry if the cake has cracked—it will all be covered up, and will still taste good! Spread the chocolate spread over the sponge. Roll up the sponge and put it on a serving plate.

8 Put the cream for the icing in a small saucepan. ASK AN ADULT TO HELP YOU heat the cream until it is steaming hot, but not boiling. Remove the pan from the heat. Break up the bittersweet chocolate and add it to the pan of hot cream. Leave for 2 minutes then stir gently until smooth and melted. Leave until the mixture is thick enough to spread, about 1 hour.

9 Spread the cooled chocolate cream all over the top and sides of your cake. Run the prongs of a fork down the log so it looks like bark on a real tree. Sprinkle with sifted confectioners' sugar "snow" then add as many decorations as you like.

10 When you are ready to eat your cake remove all of your decorations and ASK AN ADULT TO HELP YOU cut it into round slices. Your yule log is best stored in an airtight container in a cool place and eaten within 3 days.

These meringues are great with ice cream and bananas. If you can take the egg whites out of the fridge for an hour before you start, it helps a lot. A wire whisk or an electric mixer or whisk and a spotlessly clean, grease-free bowl are essential to beat the whites to a stiff snow.

chocolate meringues

Makes 12 meringues

3 oz. good bittersweet chocolate

3 egg whites, from extra-large eggs

a pinch of cream of tartar (optional)

⅞ cup superfine or granulated sugar

nonstick baking parchment
2 baking sheets

1 ASK AN ADULT TO HELP YOU preheat the oven to 250°F.

2 Cut out 2 rectangles of nonstick baking parchment to fit your baking sheets, then put one on each tray.

3 Break up the chocolate and put it in a small heatproof bowl. ASK AN ADULT TO HELP YOU melt the chocolate. Half-fill a saucepan with water, carefully put it on the stove, and bring the water to a boil. Turn off the heat, set the bowl over the pan, and leave the chocolate to melt gently, stirring every few minutes until smooth. Carefully remove the bowl from the pan and leave to cool slightly while you whisk up the whites.

4 Put the egg whites and cream of tartar, if using, in a large, spotlessly clean and grease-free bowl (grease will make it difficult to whisk the whites stiffly). Stand the bowl on a damp paper towel to keep it from wobbling.

5 Using a wire or electric whisk or mixer, start beating the egg whites. Whisk steadily until the whites turn into a stiff white foam—lift out the whisk and there will be a little peak of white standing on the end; if you are brave enough to turn the bowl upside down, the whites will remain in the bowl.

6 Tip the sugar onto the whites and whisk it into them to make a stiff and glossy meringue. Stop whisking as soon as all of the sugar has been combined.

7 Drizzle the melted chocolate over the meringue then gently stir through, using a very few strokes so the mixture looks very streaky and marbled.

8 Scoop a heaped tablespoon of mixture out of the bowl and drop it onto one of the prepared baking sheets to make a craggy heap. Repeat with the rest of the mixture to make 12, spacing them slightly apart on the baking sheets.

9 ASK AN ADULT TO HELP YOU put the meringues in the preheated oven to bake for 2 hours. ASK AN ADULT TO HELP YOU carefully remove the sheets from the oven and leave to cool. Peel the meringues off the lining paper and pile them up in a serving bowl. Your meringues can also be stored in an airtight container for up to a week.

Another idea

The meringues can also be made in the same way, then shaped into nests, by making a slight hollow in the middle of each one with the back of a spoon. After baking and cooling you can fill them with a scoop of ice cream or fruit.

This is a rich bread dough, made with milk, egg, and butter, that is rolled up with sugar, cinnamon, and pecans or raisins then cut into spiral buns. Warm from the oven, they smell and taste heavenly. The dough can be made with your hands or using a large electric mixer fitted with a special "dough hook."

sticky cinnamon buns

Makes 12 buns

For the dough:

4 cups unbleached white bread flour

1 envelope or 2½ teaspoons active dry yeast

1 teaspoon salt

3 tablespoons superfine or granulated sugar

1 extra-large egg, at room temperature

1⅓ cups milk, lukewarm

3 tablespoons unsalted butter, very soft

For the filling:

2 tablespoons butter, very soft

1 teaspoon ground cinnamon

4 tablespoons soft light brown sugar

½ cup pecan pieces or raisins

a baking sheet, very well greased

1 Put the flour in a large mixing bowl. Add the yeast, salt, and sugar and mix everything with your hand or ASK AN ADULT TO HELP YOU with the mixer dough hook. Make a hollow in the center of the flour mixture.

2 Mix the egg with the milk and add to the bowl with the butter.

3 Using your hand, slowly stir the flour into the liquid in the hollow, then work the mixture with your hand until all the flour has been mixed in. Flours vary, so if there are dry crumbs in the bowl and the dough feels dry add a little more milk, a tablespoonful at a time. If the dough is very sticky add a little more flour. If using the electric mixer use the lowest speed.

4 When the mixture comes together to make a soft dough, gather it into a ball. Sprinkle a little flour over the kitchen counter and tip the dough out of the bowl onto it. Knead the dough with both hands, stretching it out then gathering back into a ball (see pages 58–59) for 5 minutes. The dough can be kneaded using an electric mixer on low speed for 4 minutes.

5 Put the dough back into the mixing bowl and cover the bowl with a snap-on lid or put the bowl into a large, clean plastic bag and tie it closed. Leave the bowl near a warm stove or above a radiator until doubled in size—about 1 hour. It will take longer at normal room temperature or on a cool day.

6 Uncover the bowl and gently punch down the dough with your fist. Sprinkle your counter lightly with flour then tip the dough onto it.

7 Using your hands or a rolling pin, press or roll the dough out to a rectangle about 10 x 14 inches. Spread the butter for the filling over the dough. Mix the cinnamon and sugar and sprinkle over the butter. Lastly, scatter the nuts or raisins over the dough and lightly press down.

8 Roll up the dough from one of the long sides (like a Swiss roll) to make a long roll, then pinch the "seam" of the dough to seal it. ASK AN ADULT TO HELP YOU cut it into 12 equal pieces.

9 Put the rolls slightly apart on the prepared baking sheet with the cut side facing up so you can see the spiral filling. Cover the sheet with a clean, dry paper towel and leave to rise for 20 minutes. Meanwhile ASK AN ADULT TO HELP YOU preheat the oven to 425°F.

10 Uncover the buns then ASK AN ADULT TO HELP YOU put the sheet in the preheated oven to bake for 20 minutes, until golden brown. ASK AN ADULT TO HELP YOU remove the sheet from the oven. Use a metal spatula to lift the buns onto a wire rack to cool. Eat warm or at room temperature. Once they are cold you can keep your buns in an airtight container and eat them within 2 days or freeze them for up to 1 month.

This is an easy-to-make, all-in-one loaf cake flavored with fresh orange. Look out for an unwaxed orange—half of it will be whizzed up in a processor and the other half used for the topping.

fresh orange cake

Makes 1 large loaf cake

1 unwaxed orange, washed
1½ sticks unsalted butter,
     very soft
1¼ cups superfine or
     granulated sugar
3 extra large eggs,
     at room temperature
2 cups all-purpose flour
1 teaspoon bicarbonate
     of soda
½ cup milk
3 tablespoons plain yogurt
     (whole milk or low-fat, not
     fat-free)
3 tablespoons superfine or
     granulated sugar, for the
     topping

a large loaf pan,
     10 x 5 x 4 inches
nonstick baking parchment

1 ASK AN ADULT TO HELP YOU preheat the oven to 350°F. Lightly rub the inside of the loaf pan with a little soft butter on a piece of paper towel. Cut a long strip of nonstick baking parchment the same width as the pan. Press the paper into the pan so it covers the base and the two short sides.

2 Carefully cut the orange in half. Save one half for the topping. Remove the pips from the other half then cut it into 8 pieces. Put the pieces, as they are with the skin still on, in a food processor and ASK AN ADULT TO HELP YOU run the processor until the orange is chopped into very small pieces. ASK AN ADULT TO HELP YOU remove the blade from the processor then transfer the orange mixture to a mixing bowl or the bowl of an electric mixer.

3 Add the butter and sugar to the bowl. Break the eggs into a small bowl, pick out any pieces of shell, then pour the eggs into the mixing bowl.

4 Set a strainer over the bowl. Spoon the flour and bicarbonate of soda into the strainer then sift into the bowl. Add the milk and yogurt then beat with a wooden spoon or electric mixer (on low speed) for 1 minute until well mixed and there are no streaks of flour visible.

5 Spoon the mixture into the prepared pan and spread the surface to make it smooth.

6 ASK AN ADULT TO HELP YOU put the cake in the preheated oven to bake for about 50 minutes, until a good golden brown. To test if the cake is cooked ASK AN ADULT TO HELP YOU remove it from the oven, then push a toothpick into the center. If the stick comes out clean, then the loaf is ready; if it is sticky with mixture, then cook the loaf for another 5 minutes.

7 While the loaf is cooking, make the topping. Squeeze out the juice from the reserved orange half with a lemon squeezer. Pour the juice into a small bowl, add the sugar, and stir for a minute to make a thick, syrupy glaze.

8 When the loaf is cooked, ASK AN ADULT TO HELP YOU remove it from the oven and stand the pan on a wire rack. Prick the top of the loaf all over with a toothpick to make lots of small holes in it. Spoon the orange syrup all over the top so it trickles into the holes. Leave until completely cold before carefully removing the cake from the pan. Peel off the lining paper. Cut the cake into thick slices. Store your cake in an airtight container and eat it within 4 days.

This light golden sponge cake, speckled with pieces of dried fruit, is an ideal bake for several pairs of hands—there's plenty of measuring, cutting up with scissors, and mixing to do.

apricot & mango cake

Makes 1 large cake

I unwaxed orange
⅔ cup soft dried apricots
1 oz. or ¼ cup dried mango
1⅓ cup all-purpose flour
2 teaspoons baking powder
1 teaspoon ground cinnamon
¾ cup firm-packed soft light
  brown sugar
3 tablespoons sliced almonds,
  almonds
3 extra large eggs
11 tablespoons unsalted
  butter, very soft
coarse brown sugar or sliced
  almonds, for sprinkling
  (optional)

a round deep cake pan or
  springform cake pan,
  8 inches diameter
nonstick baking parchment

1 ASK AN ADULT TO HELP YOU preheat the oven to 325°F. Put a little soft butter on a piece of paper towel and rub it inside the cake pan so it is lightly coated. Stand the pan on a sheet of nonstick baking parchment, draw around the base of the pan, then cut out the circle just inside the line you have drawn. Fit the circle into the base of the pan.

2 Rinse and dry the orange. Using a fine grater, or an orange/lemon zester, grate or zest the orange peel from the orange into a small bowl, leaving the white pith on the fruit. Cut the fruit in half and squeeze out the juice using an lemon squeezer. Measure 2 tablespoons of the juice into the bowl with the zest. (You can drink the rest of the orange juice or use it for a smoothie.) Using kitchen scissors, carefully cut the apricots and mango into small pieces about the size of your thumbnail. Put them in the bowl with the juice and zest and give them a stir. Leave to soak until needed.

3 Set a strainer over a mixing bowl. Sift the flour, baking powder, cinnamon, and sugar into the bowl. Stir in the almonds.

4 Break the eggs into a small bowl. Pick out any pieces of shell then beat lightly with a fork to just break up the eggs. Tip into the mixing bowl. Put the butter into the bowl, then mix everything together with a wooden spoon until very smooth, or ASK AN ADULT TO HELP YOU mix with an electric mixer on medium speed.

5 Add the apricot mixture to the bowl and stir in gently with a wooden spoon. Spoon the mixture into the prepared pan and spread evenly. Sprinkle with sugar or sliced almonds, if using. ASK AN ADULT TO HELP YOU put the cake in the preheated oven to bake for 45–50 minutes, until a good golden brown. To test if the cake is cooked, ASK AN ADULT TO HELP YOU remove the cake from the oven, push a toothpick into the center of the cake. If the toothpick comes out clean, the cake is cooked; if there is mixture clinging to it, bake for 5 minutes more and test again. ASK AN ADULT TO HELP YOU remove the cake from the oven and leave to cool for 5 minutes. Remove from the pan and leave to cool completely on a wire rack. Store your cake in an airtight container and eat it within 5 days.

The base is like a rich, crisp shortbread, which you can make in a processor or with your hands. Save the leftover egg whites to make meringues (see page 40). For the topping you can use blueberries, apricots, cherries, or blackberries.

fresh fruit torte

Makes 1 large torte

For the base:
1¼ cups all-purpose flour
1 teaspoon baking powder
½ teaspoon ground cinnamon
¼ cup superfine or
   granulated sugar
yolks from 2 extra-large eggs
½ stick unsalted butter,
   chilled and diced
10 oz. fresh blueberries,
   blackberries, or cherries,
   or 14 oz. apricots or plums,
   rinsed

For the topping:
¼ cup all-purpose flour
¼ teaspoon ground cinnamon
2 tablespoons superfine or
   granulated sugar
⅓ cup sliced almonds, ground
2 tablespoons unsalted butter,
   chilled and diced

*a springform cake pan, about
   8 inches diameter*
nonstick baking parchment
a baking sheet

1 ASK AN ADULT TO HELP YOU preheat the oven to 350°F.

2 Grease the inside of the cake pan with a small amount of soft butter on a piece of paper towel. Cut a circle from a sheet of nonstick baking parchment—put the cake pan on the paper and draw around it. Cut inside the line so you have a circle the size of the pan. Fit it into the bottom of the pan.

3 Put the flour, baking powder, cinnamon, and sugar into the bowl of a food processor. ASK AN ADULT TO HELP YOU use the processor to mix the ingredients together. Add the egg yolks and butter to the processor. WITH ADULT HELP, work the processor to mix all the ingredients until they look like very large crumbs. You can also make the mixture without a food processor. Put all the ingredients in a mixing bowl and work them together with your fingers.

4 ASK AN ADULT TO HELP YOU remove the blade, then tip the crumbs into the cake pan and spread evenly. Press the mixture into the pan with the back of a spoon to make an even layer.

5 Scatter the blueberries or blackberries over the cake mixture. If using cherries, ASK AN ADULT TO HELP YOU remove the stones using a cherry pitter. If using apricots or plums cut in half, then twist to separate the halves of the fruit. Remove the stone then cut each half into 4 slices. Arrange the fruit over the base.

6 Put all the ingredients for the topping into the bowl of the food processor. ASK AN ADULT TO HELP YOU use the processor to mix the ingredients until they look like big bread crumbs. You can also put all the ingredients into a mixing bowl and squeeze them with your fingers until they come together in pea-size pieces.

7 Scatter the topping evenly over the fruit. Put the cake pan on a baking sheet then ASK AN ADULT TO HELP YOU put the torte in the preheated oven to bake for 35 minutes, until golden brown. ASK AN ADULT TO HELP YOU remove it from the oven. Leave to cool on a wire rack until warm, then gently unclip the pan and remove the torte. It looks good dusted with confectioners' sugar before serving. Eat warm or at room temperature with a dollop of yogurt.

A deliciously tropical cake made from canned pineapple and shredded coconut. For the freshest taste use fruit in natural juice rather than sugar syrup, and unsweetened coconut. The easy topping is made from cream cheese mixed with more pineapple.

crushed pineapple & coconut cake

Makes 1 large loaf cake

For the cake:
2⅓ cup all-purpose flour
2 teaspoons baking powder
a pinch of salt
½ teaspoon ground cinnamon
1 cup firm-packed soft light brown sugar
9 tablespoons unsalted butter, very soft
2 extra-large eggs
½ cup unsweetened shredded coconut
14 oz. can pineapple chunks or rings in natural juice

For the topping:
5 oz. full-fat cream cheese
½ cup firm packed confectioners' sugar

a loaf pan, 10 x 5 x 4 inches
nonstick baking parchment

1 ASK AN ADULT TO HELP YOU preheat the oven to 350°F. Put a little soft butter on a small piece of paper towel and rub around the inside of the pan. Cut a strip of nonstick baking parchment the same width as the pan and long enough to cover the base of the pan and both short ends. Fit the paper into the pan.

2 Set a strainer over a mixing bowl. Tip the flour, baking powder, salt, and cinnamon into the strainer and sift into the bowl. Add the sugar and mix well, breaking up any small lumps. Make a well in the center of the ingredients.

3 Put the butter into the well. Break the eggs into a small bowl, pick out any pieces of shell then tip onto the butter. Tip the coconut on top.

4 ASK AN ADULT TO HELP YOU open the can of pineapple. Set a small strainer over a jug or small bowl and drain the pineapple in the strainer. When it has drained, weigh out 5 oz. of the pineapple and chop it up or cut it into small pieces. Save the rest of the pineapple for the topping. Put the chopped pineapple in the bowl with the eggs, butter, and coconut. Measure ½ cup of the pineapple juice and pour it on top of the pineapple in the mixing bowl. Save the rest of the juice for the topping.

5 Mix together all the ingredients in the mixing bowl with a wooden spoon, until thoroughly combined. Spoon into the prepared pan and spread evenly. ASK AN ADULT TO HELP YOU put the cake in the preheated oven to bake for about 55 minutes, until golden brown. To test whether the cake is cooked, stick a toothpick into the center. If the toothpick comes out clean, then the cake is cooked; if it has sticky cake mixture on it, bake for another 5 minutes and test again. ASK AN ADULT TO HELP YOU remove the cake from the oven and leave it to cool on a wire rack. When it is completely cold, run a round-bladed knife around the inside of the pan to loosen the cake then carefully remove it from the pan.

6 To make the topping, put the cream cheese and confectioners' sugar in a small mixing bowl. Add 2 teaspoons of the leftover pineapple juice (you can treat yourself to the rest!) then beat well with a wooden spoon until smooth. Spread the mixture over the top of the cake. Decorate with some of the leftover pineapple pieces (again, you can have the rest). Serve immediately or store your cake in an airtight container in a cool place and eat it within 3 days.

raspberry shortcake

Makes 9 shortcakes

For the base:
1½ cups all-purpose flour
scant ¼ cup cornstarch
a pinch of salt
⅓ cup superfine or granulated
  sugar
5½ oz. unsalted butter,
  straight from the fridge

For the filling:
½ cup fresh raspberries
½ cup good raspberry jam

For the topping:
½ cup porridge oats
3 tablespoons light brown
  muscovado sugar

a 7-inch square cake pan

1 ASK AN ADULT TO HELP YOU preheat the oven to 350°F. Put a little soft butter on a piece of paper towel and rub it around the inside of the cake pan.

2 Tip the flour, cornstarch, salt, and sugar into the bowl of a food processor. ASK AN ADULT TO HELP YOU work the processor for a few seconds to mix the ingredients. Cut the butter into small pieces and add to the bowl of the processor. Work the processor until the mixture looks like fine crumbs. Carefully remove the lid and ASK AN ADULT TO HELP YOU remove the blade.

3 Tip the mixture into a bowl. Set aside one-third of the mixture for the topping. Tip the rest of the mixture into the prepared pan. Give the pan a shake so it is evenly spread, then press it down with your hand to make a firm, even layer. If it seems sticky, dip your fingers in a little flour. ASK AN ADULT TO HELP YOU put the shortcake base in the preheated oven to bake for 10 minutes, then remove it from the oven. Leave to cool while you make the filling and topping. Leave the oven on.

4 Put the raspberries and jam into a bowl and mix gently. Put to one side.

5 Put the shortcake crumbs that you put aside into another mixing bowl. Add the oats and sugar, mix well, then squeeze the mixture together with your hands so it comes together into flakes or large crumbs.

6 Gently spread the raspberry mixture over the baked shortcake. Scatter the oat topping evenly over the raspberries. ASK AN ADULT TO HELP YOU put the pan back into the oven and bake for another 15–20 minutes, until a light golden brown and bubbling around the edges. ASK AN ADULT TO HELP YOU remove the pan from the oven and leave to cool on a wire rack.

7 When completely cold, run a round-bladed knife around the inside of the pan then cut the shortcake into 9 squares. Store your shortcake in an airtight container and eat it within 4 days. It's also really good served with custard as a dessert.

A combination of fine Scottish foods—buttery shortcake covered with fresh raspberries and raspberry jam and then a crunchy oat topping. A bit like a very posh jam tart!

Chocolate and peanut butter are a well-loved combination—you can even buy them in a jar together! These little fairy cakes will please fans of both. But if you are cooking for a birthday party, remember to label them clearly so anyone who has an allergy to peanuts can avoid them.

little peanut butter cakes

Makes 12 small cakes

¼ cup peanut butter

2 tablespoons unsalted butter, very soft

⅔ cup firm-packed soft light brown sugar

2 extra-large eggs

½ teaspoon vanilla extract

1 cup all-purpose flour

1 teaspoon baking powder

4 tablespoons milk

½ cup bittersweet chocolate chips, plus extra for decorating

a 12-hole muffin pan lined with paper muffin cases

1 ASK AN ADULT TO HELP YOU preheat the oven to 350°F.

2 Put the peanut butter and ordinary butter in a large mixing bowl or the bowl of a food mixer. Add the sugar and beat with a wooden spoon or ASK AN ADULT TO HELP YOU use the mixer until well mixed.

3 Break the eggs into a small bowl. Pick out any pieces of shell, then add the vanilla extract and break up the eggs with a fork. Add a tablespoon of the eggs to the mixing bowl and beat well. Gradually add all of the egg mixture to the mixing bowl, beating well each time.

4 Set a strainer over the mixing bowl. Tip the flour and baking powder into the strainer and sift onto the mixture. Add the milk, then gently stir into the other ingredients. When well mixed, add the chocolate chips and mix in.

5 Spoon the mixture into the paper muffin cases until they are about one-third full. Sprinkle with chocolate chips.

6 ASK AN ADULT TO HELP YOU put the cakes in the preheated oven to bake for 15–20 minutes, until a light golden color. ASK AN ADULT TO HELP YOU remove them from the oven and leave to cool on a wire rack.

7 If you want to decorate your cakes, ASK AN ADULT TO HELP YOU cut a simple shape, such as a heart or star, out of paper to make a stencil. Hold your stencil over each cake and use a pastry brush dipped in a little milk or water to slightly moisten the area where you want the confectioners' sugar to stick. Lift off the stencil. Put some confectioners' sugar in a small strainer and shake it over the cakes. Next shake each cake and the sugar shape will appear. Magic! When cold, store your cakes in an airtight container and eat them within 4 days.

breads

making bread

Makes 1 large loaf

**5 cups unbleached white or
wholemeal bread flour
(or 2½ cups of each)**
1½ teaspoons salt
**1 envelope or 2½ teaspoons
active dry yeast**
**about 2 cups lukewarm water
or milk**

a 2 lb. loaf pan

1 Sift the flour into a large mixing bowl. Add the salt and dry yeast and mix well with your hand. You can also make the dough using a large electric mixer but ASK AN ADULT TO HELP YOU with this. Put the flour, salt, and yeast in the mixer bowl and use the dough hook attachment on the lowest speed to mix the ingredients. Make a well in the center of the flour.

2 Pour 2 cups lukewarm water into this well. Using your hands (or the dough hook) slowly stir the flour into the liquid—the mixture will turn from a thick batter to a soft dough as more flour is drawn in. Work the mixture until all the flour has been mixed in. If there are dry crumbs in the bowl and the dough feels very dry and hard to mix, add a little more water, 1 tablespoon at a time. If the dough is very sticky and sticks to your fingers or to the sides of the bowl, add a little more flour, 1 tablespoon at a time.

3 Sprinkle a little flour over the counter and tip the dough out of the bowl onto it. Using both hands, knead the dough by stretching it away from you as if pulling out a rubber band, then gather it back into a ball. Turn the ball around and stretch the dough out again then gather it back into a ball. Keep doing this for about 10 minutes until the dough is soft and smooth— it's hard work but you can take a little rest every now and then. You can also knead the dough in the mixer for 4 minutes on the lowest speed.

4 Put the kneaded dough back into the mixing bowl. It must now be left to rise. The yeast dough needs to be kept warm and moist for the yeast to thrive and do its work, so cover the bowl with a snap-on lid or put the bowl into a large, clean plastic bag and tie it closed.

How to bake a loaf of bread

Nothing tastes or smells as wonderful as your
first loaf of homemade bread. It's not difficult,
it's cheap (you only need four things—proper
bread flour, salt, yeast, and lukewarm water)
and not much can go wrong. You can kill the
yeast with too much heat—if the mixing liquid
is too hot for your little finger, it's too hot for
the yeast (it's a living fungus, believe it or not,
just "resting" in its little envelope).

Here's the basic recipe, you can make a loaf
or rolls, or add fruit and nuts or seeds.

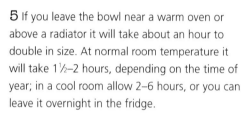

5 If you leave the bowl near a warm oven or above a radiator it will take about an hour to double in size. At normal room temperature it will take 1½–2 hours, depending on the time of year; in a cool room allow 2–6 hours, or you can leave it overnight in the fridge.

6 While the dough is rising, put some soft butter on a piece of paper towel and rub it inside the loaf pan to grease it.

7 When the dough has doubled in size, uncover the bowl and gently punch down the dough with your fist. Sprinkle the counter lightly with flour then tip the dough out onto it. Shape the dough into a brick to fit your loaf pan. Lift the dough into the pan and gently press it down.

8 Put the pan in the plastic bag and let the dough rise in a warm place until doubled in size. This should take about 1 hour.

9 ASK AN ADULT TO HELP YOU preheat the oven to 425°F. Uncover the dough and ASK AN ADULT TO HELP YOU carefully put the tin in the oven. Bake it for 35 minutes until the loaf is a good golden brown. WITH ADULT HELP, carefully remove the pan from the oven and tip the bread out of the pan onto a wire rack to cool.

10 To make sure the bread is cooked right through, carefully (the bread is very hot) tap the underside of the loaf with the back of your hand—it should sound hollow like a drum. If you hear a dull thud then put the loaf (without the pan) back in the oven for another 5 minutes then test again in the same way.

11 Leave the bread to cool completely on the wire rack before cutting. Eat your loaf within 5 days or freeze it for up to a month.

Other ideas

The same dough can be shaped into rolls instead of a loaf shape: divide the dough into 15 even pieces. Dip your hands in a little flour then roll the dough into balls, sausage shapes, twists, or animal shapes with raisins for eyes, or flatten the balls to make hamburger buns or baps. Let them rise, spaced well apart on 2 well-greased baking sheets, then bake in the preheated oven for 15–20 minutes, depending on the thickness of the rolls.

The same dough can be made into a sunflower loaf: when you make up the dough add 3 tablespoons sunflower seeds (or a ready-made seed mixture) to the flour with the salt and

yeast. Mix well then add 1 tablespoon honey to the lukewarm water and use to make the dough. While the dough is rising the first time, rub a little soft butter inside the pan then scatter a tablespoon of seeds inside the pan. When you have put the shaped dough into the loaf pan lightly brush the top with a little milk or water then scatter another tablespoon of seeds over the top. Leave to rise again then bake as above.

You can also use the dough to make a fruit loaf: add ⅓ cup superfine sugar to the flour with the salt and yeast (at Easter time you can make a hot cross bun dough by adding 1½ teaspoons

apple-pie spice as well) and ¾ cup mixed dried fruit. Mix well, then mix 1 egg with 1⅔ cup lukewarm milk and add to the bowl instead of the water to make the dough. After kneading, leave the dough to rise as above, then shape into a loaf or a large plait or into 15 buns. Leave to double in size then bake as above.

To make your bread shiny: just before baking the bread, dip a pastry brush into a little beaten egg or milk and carefully brush over the top of the dough, but don't let it drip onto the pan or the baking sheet (otherwise the dough might become "glued on" during baking).

My son Dan wanted to make a stripey loaf of bread for a school project, so he tried layering the dough with different ingredients, and this is the one we all liked the best. It's very good toasted.

red bread

Makes 1 large loaf

2¾ cups unbleached white
   bread flour
¾ cup wholemeal bread flour
   or spelt flour
1 teaspoon salt
1 x ¼ oz. envelope
   (2½ teaspoons) active
   dry yeast
about 1⅓ cups lukewarm
   water
7 oz. Monterey Jack or
   Wisconsin brick cheese,
   grated

*a nonstick baking sheet,
greased*

1 Put both flours, salt, and dry yeast in a mixing bowl and mix everything well with your hand or ASK AN ADULT TO HELP YOU put it in the bowl of an electric mixer and use the dough hook attachment.

2 Pour the lukewarm water into the bowl and mix with the flour using your hand, or on low speed if using a mixer, to make a soft dough. If there are dry crumbs at the bottom of the bowl that won't mix in, add more water 1 tablespoon at a time. If the dough is sticky and clings to your hands or the bowl, work in a little more flour.

3 Sprinkle a little flour over the kitchen counter and tip the dough out onto it. Using both hands, knead the dough by stretching it away from you then gathering it back into a ball again. Keep doing this for about 10 minutes. You can also knead the dough in the mixer—it will take 4 minutes at very low speed.

4 Put the kneaded dough back into the mixing bowl—it now has to be left to rise. Cover the bowl with a snap-on lid or put the bowl into a large clean plastic bag and tie it closed. Leave the bowl near a warm oven or radiator for about an hour or until the dough has doubled in size.

5 Uncover the risen dough and gently punch down the dough with your fist. Sprinkle the work surface with flour then tip the dough out onto it. Using a rolling pin, roll out the dough away from you to a long thin rectangle, 7 x 16 inches. Sprinkle the grated cheese over the

bottom two thirds of the dough, leaving the top third of the dough uncovered. Gently press the cheese onto the dough to make an even layer.

6 You now have to fold the dough into three, like an envelope. Fold the top uncovered portion of dough down to cover the center portion of dough. Now fold up the bottom portion of dough to cover the rest of the dough—to make three layers of dough. Have a rest for 5 minutes.

7 Roll out the dough to a rectangle again and repeat step 6 (without adding more cheese) to make 9 layers of dough. Do this step once more and you should now have 27 layers of dough!

8 Use your hands to roll the dough into a sausage about 24 inches long, then tie a knot or make the sausage a bit longer and cut it into 3 then plait together. Set on the baking sheet.

9 Cover the dough by slipping the sheet into a plastic bag or covering it with a clean, slightly damp kitchen towel. Leave to rise in a warm place for about 50 minutes, until almost doubled in size. ASK AN ADULT TO HELP YOU preheat the oven to 425°F.

10 Uncover the bread and ASK AN ADULT TO HELP YOU put it in the preheated oven to bake for about 30 minutes, until golden brown. ASK AN ADULT TO HELP YOU carefully remove the baking sheet from the oven and transfer the bread to a wire rack to cool. When cold, store it in an airtight container and eat it within 3 days.

A fun way to make a loaf—the dough is divided into small pieces then dipped in melted butter, rolled in cinnamon sugar and nuts, then piled into a loaf pan. A delicious treat!

monkey bread

Makes 1 large loaf

4 cups unbleached strong white bread flour

1 teaspoon salt

1 x ¼ oz. envelope (2½ teaspoons) active dry yeast

3 tablespoons superfine or granulated sugar

4 tablespoons unsalted butter, melted

1 extra large egg, at room temperature

1 cup lukewarm milk

½ teaspoon vanilla extract

1 cup pecan pieces

4 tablespoons soft dark brown sugar

2 teaspoons ground cinnamon

4 tablespoons unsalted butter, melted

a 2 lb. loaf pan, well-greased

1 Put the flour, salt, dry yeast, and superfine sugar in a large mixing bowl. Mix everything together with your hands. Make a well in the center of the mixture.

2 Pour the melted butter into the well. Break the egg into a small bowl and pick out any pieces of shell. Beat with a fork just to break up the egg. Pour into the well with the lukewarm milk and vanilla extract. Use your hands to mix the flour into the liquids in the center—the mixture will turn from a thick batter to a dough as more flour is drawn in. Work the mixture with your hand until you have a soft, smooth dough. If there are dry crumbs and the dough feels dry and hard to work, gradually add a little more milk, 1 tablespoon at a time.

3 Scatter a little flour over the clean counter. Tip the dough out onto it and knead the dough by stretching it away from you then gathering t back into a ball. Keep doing this for about 5 minutes until the dough feels very springy and smooth. You can also make and knead the dough in a large electric mixer with a dough hook attachment—it will take 4 minutes to knead on very low speed. ASK AN ADULT TO HELP YOU with this.

4 Put the kneaded dough back into the mixing bowl—it now has to be left to rise. Cover the bowl with a snap-on lid or put the bowl into a large clean plastic bag and tie it closed.

5 Leave in a warm place, near the oven or a radiator, until doubled in size—for about 1 hour. It will take longer in a cooler place. Uncover the bowl and gently punch down the dough with your fist to knock out the air. Remove from bowl.

6 Scatter a little flour over the work surface then divide the dough into 32 even pieces—you can do this by pulling off small lumps or by shaping the dough into a log and cutting it in half then keep dividing it until you have 32 pieces.

7 Put the pecan pieces, brown sugar, and cinnamon in a small bowl and mix well. Dip a piece of dough into the melted butter then into the nut mixture and put in the prepared pan. Keep doing this until all the pieces of dough have been dipped and put in the pan. They do not have to be arranged too neatly, they can look quite higgledy-piggledy and there can be gaps in between them. Cover the loaf pan with a clean, dry kitchen towel and leave to rise in a warm place for 40 minutes. While the dough is rising, ASK AN ADULT TO HELP YOU preheat the oven to 400°F.

8 Uncover the pan and again, WITH ADULT HELP, put it into the preheated oven to bake for 30 minutes, until golden brown. ASK AN ADULT TO HELP YOU remove it from the oven and leave for 5 minutes before turning out onto a wire rack. Serve warm. Store your bread in an airtight container and eat it within 4 days.

tomato pesto rolls

Makes 10 small rolls

4 cups self-rising flour

½ teaspoon salt

8 oz. natural cottage cheese (no additives)

a small bunch of fresh basil, save 10 leaves for decoration

1 extra large egg

about ⅔ cup whole or half-fat milk

5 cherry tomatoes, halved

2 tablespoons pesto (basil pesto or sun-dried tomato pesto) or olive oil

a nonstick baking sheet

1 ASK AN ADULT TO HELP YOU preheat the oven to 375°F. Sprinkle a little flour over the baking sheet and put it to one side.

2 Put the flour, salt, cottage cheese, and basil into the bowl of a food processor. WITH ADULT HELP, run the machine until the ingredients are just mixed, and look like crumbs.

3 Break the egg into a jug, pick out any pieces of shell then add ⅔ cup milk and beat with a fork, just to combine the egg and milk.

4 WITH ADULT HELP, run the machine and pour in the egg/milk mix through the feed tube. Stop the processor when the ingredients have come together to make a ball of soft dough. If there are dry crumbs and the dough feels hard and dry, add a little more milk.

5 Sprinkle a little flour over the counter. ASK AN ADULT to remove the processor blade then turn out the dough onto the counter. Flour your hands, then gently work and knead the dough twice so it looks smoother.

6 Divide the dough into 10 equal pieces and shape each into a ball. Arrange the balls slightly apart on the prepared baking sheet. Make a deep hole in the center of each with your finger. Push a basil leaf into each hole then a tomato half—cut-side up. Make sure the tomato is deep in the hole in the dough (or it will pop right out during baking!). Brush the top of each roll with the pesto or olive oil.

7 ASK AN ADULT TO HELP YOU put the rolls in the preheated oven to bake for about 20 minutes, until they are golden brown. ASK AN ADULT TO

Here the dough is mixed in a food processor for speed, though you can also make it with your hands. It is made with cottage cheese, which is packed with calcium and good for your bones and teeth. I've given recipes for two flavors—one with tomatoes and pesto and a sweet version, with honey and fresh or dried fruits.

HELP YOU take the rolls out of the oven and carefully put them on a wire rack. Leave to cool until just warm. Eat immediately or the same day. They can also be split in half and toasted the next day, or frozen for up to 1 month.

To make sweet fruit rolls
Follow the recipe opposite but leave out the basil, tomatoes, and pesto or oil. Instead, add 1 tablespoon of clear honey to the processor with the cottage cheese mixture. Make the dough as for the method opposite, then turn it out onto the counter. Scatter 3 tablespoons of fresh blueberries, or 2 tablespoons of dried cherries or chopped, ready-to-eat dried apricots over the dough and knead them into it. Shape into 10 rolls and arrange on the baking sheet then ASK AN ADULT TO HELP YOU put them in the preheated oven to bake for about 20 minutes.

The traditional bread of rural Ireland was made at home, and baked in a heavy iron pot set over a peat fire. The breads were quickly made—no kneading or rising—and the light texture comes from mixing the flour with buttermilk, which is acidic and reacts with the alkaline bicarbonate of soda to make bubbles of carbon dioxide. Soda bread is best eaten on the day it is baked.

irish soda bread

Makes 1 medium loaf

White soda bread
3½ cups all-purpose
    white flour
1 teaspoon salt
1¼ teaspoons bicarbonate
    of soda
about 1½ cups buttermilk
    (or ¾ cup each plain yogurt
    and milk)

a nonstick baking sheet

1 ASK AN ADULT TO HELP YOU preheat the oven to 425°F. Scatter a little flour over the baking sheet and put to one side.

2 Set a large strainer over a large mixing bowl. Tip the flour into the strainer, add the salt and bicarbonate of soda, and sift into the bowl. Make a well in the center.

3 Pour the buttermilk into the well. Mix everything together with a round-bladed table knife, or with your hands, to make a soft and slightly sticky dough. Don't worry if it looks a bit rough.

4 Scatter a little flour onto your kitchen counter, then turn out the dough onto it. Dust your hands with flour then gently shape the dough into a ball.

5 Set the ball of dough on the prepared baking sheet and flatten it slightly so it is 1¼–1½ inches high. Using the same table knife, score the dough into 4 quarters.

6 ASK AN ADULT TO HELP YOU put the loaf in the preheated oven to bake for about 35 minutes, until a good golden brown. ASK AN ADULT TO

HELP YOU remove it from the oven and tip it upside down onto a wire rack, then tap the underside with your knuckles. The loaf is cooked if it sounds hollow. If it sounds like a dull "thud" bake it for 5 minutes more. Leave on the wire rack until cool enough to slice.

For speckled white soda bread: Add 4 oz. chopped bittersweet chocolate or chocolate chips, and 1 tablespoon superfine sugar to the bowl with the sifted flour. Mix then finish the recipe as above.

For brown soda bread: The coarse brown wheaten flour traditionally used is hard to find outside Ireland, but a mix of plain wholemeal flour (stoneground if possible), white flour, and wheatbran and wheatgerm (from wholefood shops) works well. To make a brown loaf, replace the white flour in the recipe for white soda bread (see left) with 1½ cups all-purpose white flour, 1½ cups wholemeal flour, and ¾ cup wheatbran and wheatgerm mix. Follow the recipe by mixing all the dry ingredients together (but don't sift them into the bowl), then mix to a soft dough with the buttermilk. Shape and bake the loaf as for the white soda bread loaf.

Unlike most bread doughs that need a lot of kneading for a good texture, this one is dead simple. The good, brioche-like taste, texture, and smell come from the Swiss cheese plus eggs, yet the dough is mixed in the bowl with your hands or with a large electric mixer and left to rise just once, in the pan, before baking. Eat it thickly sliced with tomato soup or salads or use for sandwiches, toast, or grilled cheese sandwiches.

no-knead cheese bread

Makes 1 large loaf

4 cups unbleached white
   bread flour
1½ teaspoons salt
¼ teaspoon freshly ground
   black pepper
¼ teaspoon mustard powder
   (optional)
a good pinch of cayenne
   pepper (or a little more if
   you like it spicy)
1 x ¼ oz. envelope
   (2½ teaspoons) active
   dry yeast
4 oz. Swiss cheese, grated
4 extra-large eggs, at room
   temperature
1 cup whole milk, lukewarm
   (read method, right)

a 2 lb. loaf pan

1 Put a little soft butter on a piece of paper towel and rub it around the inside of the pan.

2 Put the flour in a large mixing bowl, or the bowl of a large electric mixer. Add the salt, black pepper, mustard powder, cayenne pepper, and dry yeast. Mix all these ingredients well with your hand, or WITH ADULT HELP, the dough hook attachment of the mixer.

3 Mix in the grated cheese then make a well in the center of the ingredients. Break the eggs into a small bowl, pick out any pieces of shell, then beat with a fork just to break up the eggs. Pour into the well in the flour mixture.

4 To encourage the yeast to grow and produce the carbon dioxide that makes your dough rise it is ideal to use lukewarm milk, about the same temperature as your body. If the milk is too hot the yeast will be killed, if it is too cool then they will take a long time to become active. Gently heat the milk in a small pan over low heat, or in the microwave. Dip your finger into the milk—it should feel just warm and comfortable, not too hot or too chilly. Pour the milk onto the eggs.

5 Using your hand, or WITH ADULT HELP, the dough hook attachment (use the lowest speed on the mixer) work the flour into the eggs

and milk to make a soft and sticky dough. Mix the dough in the bowl for 2 minutes, until the dough leaves the sides of the bowl clean.

6 Scrape the dough out of the bowl into the prepared pan and press it evenly into the pan. If it feels very sticky, dip your fingers into a little flour.

7 Put the bowl into a large clean plastic bag and tie it closed, making sure the bag is slightly inflated so the plastic doesn't stick to the dough. Leave to rise in a warm spot until doubled in size and just about reaching the top of the pan, about 1½–2 hours, depending on the room temperature. ASK AN ADULT TO HELP YOU preheat the oven to 375°F.

8 Uncover the dough and ASK AN ADULT TO HELP YOU put the loaf in the preheated oven to bake for 45–50 minutes, until golden brown. To test if the loaf is cooked, ASK AN ADULT TO HELP YOU remove it from the oven and tip it out of the pan upside down onto a wire rack. Tap the base of the loaf with your knuckles—if it sounds hollow like a drum, the loaf is cooked; but if it sounds like a dull "thud," then you need to cook the loaf for another 5 minutes. When ready, leave to cool on the wire rack. Eat your loaf within 4 days or freeze it for up to 1 month.

This is an Italian bread with a tasty filling, to eat with salad or soup. I've given you some ideas for the filling, but it's fun to experiment and find out what you like best.

stuffed focaccia

Makes 1 large loaf

For the dough:
5 cups unbleached white bread flour
1 x ¼ oz. envelope (2½ teaspoons) active dry yeast
1½ teaspoons salt
½ teaspoon dried mixed herbs
1¾–2 cups lukewarm water
2 tablespoons olive oil

For the filling:
4 oz. thinly sliced Italian pepperoni or Spanish chorizo, or ham
1 jar (9–10 oz.), roasted or grilled sweet peppers or sun-dried tomatoes in oil
7 oz. feta cheese or mild goat cheese
2–3 tablespoons olive oil

a small nonstick roasting pan, about 9 x 12 inches

1 Tip the flour into a large mixing bowl or ASK AN ADULT TO HELP YOU put it in the bowl of an electric mixer. Add the dry yeast, salt, and herbs and mix well with your hands or ASK AN ADULT TO HELP YOU with the dough hook attachment of the electric mixer.

2 Make a well in the center and pour in the lukewarm water and the olive oil. Gradually work the flour into the liquid with your hands or the dough hook set on low speed.

3 When the mixture comes together to make a ball of soft dough that leaves the sides of the bowl clean, scatter a little flour on your counter and tip the dough out onto it. Knead the dough for 10 minutes: first use the heel of your hand to stretch the dough away from you as if pulling out a rubber band, then gather it back into a ball. Turn the dough around and repeat the stretching out and gathering back process until the dough feels very smooth and elastic. You can also knead the dough in the mixer for 5 minutes on low speed. Put the dough ball into the bowl and leave it to rest while you make the filling.

4 Separate the slices of pepperoni, chorizo, or ham, and remove any outer skin from the pepperoni. Drain the peppers (saving the oil), then carefully cut into thick slices. Drain the cheese, if necessary, then cut into small cubes. Brush the inside of the pan with a little olive oil.

5 Divide the dough in half. Pat and stretch one piece of the dough to a rectangle the same size as the prepared pan. Fit the dough into the pan, pressing it into the corners.

6 Cover the dough with the slices of pepperoni, chorizo, or ham, then scatter the peppers over, then finally top with the cubes of cheese.

7 Press out the remaining piece of dough to a rectangle the size of the pan then gently lay it over the filling. Press it down very gently then seal the edges of the two pieces of dough by pinching them with your fingers. Carefully prick the top of the loaf all over with a toothpick or skewer to get rid of any air bubbles trapped between the layers. Slide the tin into a large plastic bag, inflate the bag slightly so the plastic doesn't stick to the dough then tie it closed. Leave for 1 hour in a warm spot so the dough almost doubles in size.

8 While the dough is rising, ASK AN ADULT TO HELP YOU preheat the oven to 425°F.

9 Uncover the risen dough and brush with the saved pepper oil or the rest of the olive oil. ASK AN ADULT TO HELP YOU put the focaccia in the preheated oven to bake for 25 minutes, until golden brown. ASK AN ADULT TO HELP YOU remove the pan from the oven and carefully turn it out onto a wire rack to cool. Eat your focaccia warm or at room temperature on the same day.

savory things

French toast is usually made from bread soaked in a sweet egg and milk mix then fried in butter, but this savory version is more nutritious and makes a good snack.

canadian french toast

Serves 4–6

½ baguette or French stick (can be a bit stale)
4 extra-large eggs
1½ cups whole milk or half and half
freshly ground black pepper
6 oz. thin sliced rindless smoked streaky bacon
4 oz. Swiss cheese, grated

a large shallow ovenproof baking dish, about 4 pints capacity

1 ASK AN ADULT TO HELP YOU preheat the oven to 400°F. Lightly rub the inside of the baking dish with a little soft butter on a piece of paper towel. Put it to one side.

2 Carefully cut the bread into slices about 1 inch thick, then fit the slices into the prepared dish like a jigsaw puzzle, slightly squashing them so that they fit together tightly.

3 Break the eggs into a mixing bowl. Pick out any pieces of shell. Pour in the milk, then add several grinds of black pepper, at least 3 but up to 6 if you like your food a bit hot. With a wire whisk, beat the mixture until it looks very frothy.

4 Pour the egg mixture evenly over the bread. Snip the rashers of bacon in half with kitchen scissors, then arrange the bacon over the top of the bread. Scatter the grated cheese evenly over the top.

5 ASK AN ADULT TO HELP YOU put the Canadian French toast in the preheated oven to bake for about 20 minutes, until golden. ASK AN ADULT TO HELP YOU carefully remove the dish from the oven and eat at once.

breakfast kabobs

Makes 4 kabobs

**8 cherry tomatoes or baby
  plum tomatoes**
½ red bell pepper
½ green bell pepper
½ yellow bell pepper
**8 small sausages or small
  frankfurters**
4 rashers back bacon
1 small red onion
**4 soft wholemeal rolls or
  hamburger buns**

4 wooden skewers
a large roasting pan, greased

1 ASK AN ADULT TO HELP YOU preheat the oven to 425°F. Soak the wooden skewers in warm water for 10 minutes. Be careful with these as they have sharp ends.

2 Meanwhile prepare the vegetables: rinse the tomatoes and peppers in cold running water, and drain well in a colander. Leave the tomatoes whole. Pull out any core and seeds from the peppers. ASK AN ADULT TO HELP YOU cut each piece of pepper into quarters using a small sharp knife.

3 Using kitchen scissors, snip the links between the sausages. Cut each rasher of bacon in half, then roll up. Peel the papery skin off the onion then WITH ADULT HELP, cut it into quarters.

4 Thread the tomatoes, peppers, sausages, bacon, and onion onto the wooden skewers, making sure there is a small gap between each piece on the skewer. You can put them in any order you like, but make sure each skewer has an equal amount of each ingredient.

5 Arrange the skewers in the prepared roasting pan, slightly apart. ASK AN ADULT TO HELP YOU put the kabobs in the preheated oven to bake for 15–20 minutes, until golden. Meanwhile ASK AN ADULT TO HELP YOU warm the bread rolls or hamburger buns, either in the toaster or in a second oven on low temperature. ASK AN ADULT TO HELP YOU remove the kabobs from the roasting pan (you might find kitchen tongs helpful) and put a kabob on each serving plate. Serve immediately with the warmed bread.

My son Dan came up with this recipe for a school project on healthy breakfasts and brunches. The onion can be replaced with a large flat field mushroom (quartered). You could add scrambled eggs and a glass of orange juice.

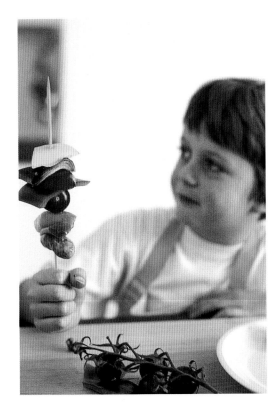

These deliciously crumbly and flaky pastry straws are given extra flavor with cheese, mustard, and a red spice called paprika. They make a tasty and filling snack any time of day. You could also make the fruity salad recipe I've given here and serve it with the straws (still warm from the oven) as an appetizer before you eat your dinner.

giant cheese straws

Makes 18 cheese straws

For the straws:
12 oz. pack ready-rolled puff pastry
2 tablespoons grainy mustard (or mild mustard)
1 teaspoon mild paprika
3½ oz. or ⅔ cup grated Parmesan cheese

For the salad:
6 slices seedless watermelon, (about 2 lb. or half a small watermelon)
7 oz. feta cheese
3–4 oz. bag ready-washed watercress (or salad leaves)
2 tablespoons olives

2 nonstick baking sheets, well greased

1 Let the pastry defrost if it is frozen. Unwrap and gently unroll and flatten the sheet of pastry It should measure about 9 x 14 inches. If your pastry is a different size don't worry. As long as you can cut it into strips about ¾ inch wide and about 8 inches long, it will work.

2 Mix the mustard with the paprika and spread evenly over the pastry. Sprinkle the cheese in an even layer over the top then gently press the cheese onto the pastry.

3 Cut the pastry into 18 even strips each 9 inches long. Take one strip and hold an end in each hand then twist the straw toward the middle. Put down onto the kitchen counter and gently roll it as if making a sausage from play dough, so the twist picks up any cheese that has dropped off, and is tightly twisted.

4 Put the twist on one of the prepared baking sheets and make the rest in the same way.

5 Chill the straws in the fridge for 15 minutes. Meanwhile, ASK AN ADULT TO HELP YOU preheat the oven to 400°F.

6 ASK AN ADULT TO HELP YOU put the cheese straws on the baking sheets into the preheated oven to bake for about 15 minutes, until golden brown and crispy.

7 ASK AN ADULT TO HELP YOU remove the sheets from the oven. Leave the straws to cool on the trays for 5 minutes then carefully lift the straws onto a wire rack using a metal spatula, and leave to cool completely. Eat as soon as possible or store in an airtight container for up to 2 days.

8 To make the salad, ASK AN ADULT TO HELP YOU cut away the rind from the watermelon slices. Carefully cut the watermelon into cubes about 1 inch in size. Drain the feta cheese if necessary then cut it into cubes the same size as the watermelon pieces.

9 Put the watercress into a salad bowl. Scatter the watermelon and feta on top then finally the olives. Eat the salad as soon as possible with the cheese straws.

crostini

Makes 4 crostini

4 large thick slices bread
12 cherry tomatoes or baby
   plum tomatoes
4 fresh basil leaves
8 pitted black olives
3 tablespoons olive oil
freshly ground black pepper
1 large garlic clove

a large baking sheet

1 ASK AN ADULT TO HELP YOU preheat the oven to its hottest setting, usually 475°F. Arrange the slices of bread on the baking sheet. ASK AN ADULT TO HELP YOU put the bread in the preheated oven to bake for 5 minutes, until golden brown. ASK AN ADULT TO HELP YOU remove the sheet from the oven and put the bread slices onto serving plates.

2 While the bread is baking, rinse the tomatoes in cold running water and drain well. ASK AN ADULT TO HELP YOU cut the tomatoes into quarters. Put into a small mixing bowl. Tear up the basil leaves into little pieces and add to the tomatoes. Quarter the olives and add to the bowl with the olive oil and black pepper. Stir gently to mix.

3 Slice the garlic clove in half and rub the cut sides over the hot bread slices. Spoon the tomato mixture over the bread and eat straightaway.

Some more ideas

Drain a small (7 oz.) can tuna and flake the fish with a fork. Arrange on top of the tomato mixture.

Cut a 5 oz. ball mozzarella cheese into small cubes. Arrange on top of the tomato mixture.

Top the tomato mixture with arugula leaves and 3½ oz. thinly sliced prosciutto.

Drain a small (7 oz.) can tuna and WITH ADULT HELP, put it in the bowl of a food processor with 2 anchovy fillets, the juice of a lemon, 2 tablespoons mayonnaise, and several grinds of black pepper. WITH ADULT HELP process to make a thick paste and spread over the bread.

This warm snack is very quick to make. Slices of bread are baked in the oven to make them crispy, then rubbed with garlic and topped with a tomato mixture. You will need good bread—try a baguette that is at least a day old, or an Italian country-style bread like *pane pugliese* or *pane rustica*.

Good for parties and picnics, as well as lunch boxes, these savory muffins are filled with molten cheese and spicy Spanish sausage.

chorizo & cheese muffins

Makes 12 muffins

4 cups all-purpose flour
2 teaspoons baking powder
a pinch of salt
freshly ground black pepper
8 oz. Swiss cheese
4 oz. thickly sliced chorizo
    sausage (or ham, or
    canned or frozen
    sweetcorn kernels)
2 extra-large eggs
7 tablespoons unsalted butter
1½ cups whole milk

*12-hole muffin pan lined with
   paper muffin cases*

1 ASK AN ADULT TO HELP YOU preheat the oven to 400°F.

2 Set a large strainer over a mixing bowl. Tip the flour into the strainer, then add the baking powder, salt, and a few grinds of pepper, and sift these ingredients into the bowl.

3 ASK AN ADULT TO HELP YOU carefully cut the cheese into small cubes. Add these to the bowl. Using kitchen scissors, cut up the chorizo into pieces about the same size as the cheese. Add to the bowl and mix well. Make a well in the center of the mixture.

4 Break the eggs into a bowl. Pick out any pieces of shell then beat the eggs with a fork until just broken up. Pour into the well in the mixture in the mixing bowl.

5 Put the butter in a small saucepan and ASK AN ADULT TO HELP YOU melt the butter over very low heat. The butter can also be melted in a microwave. Pour into the well in the mixture in the mixing bowl, along with the milk.

6 Mix all the ingredients together with a wooden spoon to make a rough-looking mixture. Spoon this mixture into the prepared muffin cases, making sure there is the same amount in each one.

7 ASK AN ADULT TO HELP YOU put the muffins in the preheated oven to bake for 30 minutes, until golden brown. ASK AN ADULT TO HELP YOU remove the pan from the oven, leave to cool for a couple of minutes then transfer the muffins to a wire rack and leave to cool completely. Eat warm or at room temperature the same or the next day and store in an airtight container.

A frittata is an Italian omelet, and this one is full of vegetables plus cheese. Instead of making the frittatas in a large skillet, try baking them in a muffin pan to make 12 small ones—perfect if you are having friends over (allow one per person for an appetizer, or two or even three for an entrée). Good with salad leaves and potato salad.

mini vegetable frittatas

Makes 12 mini frittatas

4 scallions

3 medium zucchini

1 medium red bell pepper

3½ oz. or about 1 cup loose-
   packed soft sun-dried
   tomatoes

4 oz. Swiss cheese

8 extra-large eggs

½ cup light cream or half
   and half

freshly ground black pepper

2 tablespoons olive oil

a good pinch of dried oregano

*12-hole muffin pan, well
   greased or 12 flexible
   muffin molds*
a baking sheet

1 ASK AN ADULT TO HELP YOU preheat the oven to 350°F. WITH ADULT HELP and using a small sharp knife, carefully trim the hairy root ends off the scallions, and the dark green leafy tops. Rinse the scallions well in cold running water and drain thoroughly. Slice into thin rounds then put to one side.

2 Rinse the zucchini, then trim off the ends. Slice each zucchini in half lengthwise then cut each half in half lengthwise so you have 4 long strips from each zucchini. Cut the strips across to make ½ inch pieces. Put with the scallions.

3 Rinse the red pepper. Cut off the stalk end, cut the pepper in half, and pull out the core with its seeds. Slice the pepper into strips about ½ inch wide, then cut each strip across to make ¼ inch pieces. Add to the scallions.

4 Cut the sun-dried tomatoes into ½ inch pieces but keep separate from the onion mixture.

5 Cut the cheese into ½ inch cubes and add to the tomatoes.

6 Break the eggs into a bowl. Pick out any pieces of shell. Pour the cream into the bowl, add several grinds of black pepper then, using a table fork, gently beat the eggs and cream together until thoroughly mixed.

7 Spoon the olive oil into a medium skillet. ASK AN ADULT TO HELP YOU gently heat it on the stove. Put the scallions, zucchini, red pepper, and a good pinch of oregano into the pan and stir well with a wooden spoon. Turn up the heat to medium and cook for 5 minutes, stirring carefully every minute, until the vegetables are a light golden brown. ASK AN ADULT TO HELP YOU remove the pan from the heat and put it onto a heatproof counter.

8 Leave to cool for 5 minutes then stir in the tomatoes and cheese.

9 Set the muffin pan on a baking sheet. Spoon the vegetable and cheese mixture into the holes, filling each one with an equal amount. Using a small ladle or spoon, pour the egg mix over the vegetable mixture (you may find it easier to transfer the egg mix to a large jug then pour the mix onto the vegetables).

10 ASK AN ADULT TO HELP YOU put the frittatas in the preheated oven to bake for 25 minutes, until puffed, golden, and set. WITH ADULT HELP, remove from the oven. Leave to cool for 5 minutes then gently run a round-bladed knife around the inside of each muffin hole. Carefully lift out or tip out onto a serving platter. Serve warm or at room temperature.

Full of flavor, color, and fragrant spices, this is a mild rather than a hot vegetable chili, made with butter beans and kidney beans, plus plenty of vegetables.

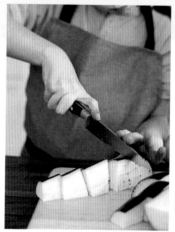 

vegetable chili

Serves 4–6

1 medium red onion
1 medium eggplant
1 red bell pepper
1 green bell pepper
2 tablespoons olive oil
2 teaspoons mild chili powder
2 teaspoons ground cumin
2 teaspoons ground coriander
1 teaspoon dried oregano
salt and freshly ground
    black pepper
2 x 14 oz. cans chopped
    tomatoes
1 x 14 oz. can red kidney
    beans in water
1 x 14 oz. can butter beans
    in water

To serve:
a few sprigs of fresh cilantro
a small tub of sour cream
cooked rice or flour tortillas

*a large flameproof, ovenproof
    casserole with lid*

1 ASK AN ADULT TO HELP YOU preheat the oven to 350°F.

2 Peel the onion to remove the papery outer skin. WITH ADULT HELP, using a small sharp knife, cut the onion in half from top to bottom. Set the halves on the cutting board flat-side down and carefully cut into thin slices. Put on one side.

3 Rinse the eggplant and both peppers in cold running water and drain. Trim the ends off the eggplant then carefully slice it in half from top to bottom. Set the halves on the cutting board cut or flat-side down. Cut each half into 5 long thin strips from top to bottom then cut these strips across every ½ inch. Set aside.

4 Cut the stalks off the peppers, then slice the peppers in half from top to bottom and pull out the cores and seeds. Cut the peppers into pieces about the same size as the eggplant.

5 Spoon the olive oil into the casserole. ASK AN ADULT TO HELP YOU put the casserole on the stove and heat gently. Add the onions to the casserole and stir with a wooden spoon. Cook gently for 10 minutes until the onions are softened. Spoon the chili powder, cumin,

coriander, oregano, and a little salt and black pepper into the casserole and stir well. Cook gently for 2 minutes, then stir again. Put the eggplant into the casserole and stir until they are coated in the onion and spice mix. Add the peppers and stir just to mix.

6 ASK AN ADULT TO HELP YOU carefully open the cans of tomatoes and add to the casserole, then stir well. Open the cans of beans and drain thoroughly in a colander.

7 Stir the beans into the casserole. It might seem that there are a lot, but the vegetables will cook down and release their juices.

8 Cover with the lid and ASK AN ADULT TO HELP YOU put the casserole in the preheated oven to bake for 1 hour. ASK AN ADULT TO HELP YOU carefully remove the casserole from the oven, remove the lid, and stir gently. Taste and add more salt and pepper (or chili) if you think it needs some. Decorate with fresh cilantro sprigs and serve with sour cream, plus rice or warm flour tortillas.

pizza and calzone

Makes 4 pizzas or calzones

For the dough:
2¾ cups all-purpose flour

1 teaspoon salt

1 x ¼ oz. envelope (2½ teaspoons) active dry yeast

1 teaspoon dried mixed herbs

1 cup plus 2 tablespoons lukewarm water

1 tablespoon olive oil

For the topping or filling:
8 oz. cherry or baby tomatoes

1 small red bell pepper

5 oz. mozzarella cheese balls

2 tablespoons olive oil

2 garlic cloves

a small bunch of basil

freshly ground black pepper

2 tablespoons pitted olives

thin-sliced salami or chorizo, anchovies, or sweetcorn

2 nonstick baking sheets, greased, or 4 metal pizza pans

1 Make the dough first: put the flour, salt, dried yeast, and dried herbs in a mixing bowl and mix well with your hands. Make a well in the dough, then pour the lukewarm water and oil into the well. Gradually work the flour into the liquids to make a soft dough. Flours vary, so if there are dry crumbs in the bowl or the dough feels stiff and dry add more water, 1 tablespoon at a time. If the dough is very sticky and clings to your fingers or the bowl, work in a little more flour. Sprinkle a little flour onto the counter and tip the dough out onto it. Now knead the dough by stretching it away from you then gathering it back into a ball. Do this for 5–10 minutes until the dough feels really smooth and elastic. The dough can also be mixed and kneaded using a large electric mixer fitted with a dough hook. ASK AN ADULT TO HELP YOU mix the dough on low speed and then knead it for 2–5 minutes.

2 Return the dough to the mixing bowl and cover the bowl with a snap-on lid or slip the bowl into a large clean plastic bag, then put the bowl in a warm place for the dough to rise until doubled in size—this will take about 1 hour.

3 ASK AN ADULT TO HELP YOU preheat the oven to 400°F. Uncover the risen dough and punch it down with your fist to deflate it. Flour the work surface again and tip the dough out onto it. Divide the dough into four equal portions. Using your floured fingers or a rolling pin, press, pull, or roll out each piece of dough to a fairly thin circle about 9 inches across. Leave to rest while you make the filling or topping.

4 Rinse the cherry tomatoes and pepper. Cut each tomato in half. Cut the pepper in half and carefully cut away the core with its seeds, and the stem, then cut the pepper into strips. Drain the mozzarella. Thinly slice the mozzarella or pull it into shreds using your fingers.

5 Pour the olive oil into a small bowl. Peel and crush the garlic and add it to the oil. Snip the basil leaves with kitchen scissors and stir in with plenty of black pepper.

6 To assemble: put a teaspoon or so of the oil mixture onto each circle of dough and spread evenly over the dough.

Homemade pizzas taste so good, and they are less greasy than most ready-made ones. A calzone is a type of pizza that's folded with a filling and it's a lot of fun to make!

7 For pizzas: arrange the circles of dough on the prepared baking sheets or metal pizza pans then arrange the tomatoes cut-side up on the circles of dough, leaving a 1 inch border of dough all around the edges. Top with the strips of pepper, cheese, and olives, plus any of the extra toppings that you want to use.

8 For calzone: arrange the tomatoes cut-side up on one half of each circle of dough leaving a 1 inch border of dough all around. Top with the strips of pepper and the cheese, then the olives. Add any of the extra toppings that you like. Brush the edges of the dough with a little water then fold the dough over the filling to cover it. Press and pinch the edges together with your fingers to firmly seal in the filling. Put the calzones on the prepared baking sheets.

9 ASK AN ADULT TO HELP YOU put your pizzas or calzones in the preheated oven to bake. This will take 15–20 minutes for the pizzas and 25 minutes for the calzones. The calzone is ready when it is a golden brown color. When your pizzas or calzones are ready, ASK AN ADULT TO HELP YOU remove them from the oven and leave to cool for a few minutes before eating. Take care when you eat your calzones as the filling will be very hot!

Risotto is usually made on top of
the stove, with hot liquid gradually
being stirred into the rice. I have
cheated in this recipe as all the
ingredients are cooked together
in the oven, but the result is a
very easy and tasty one-pot meal.

oven risotto with tomatoes, peas, & tuna

Serves 4–5

4 scallions

2 garlic cloves

2 x 6 oz. cans tuna in oil or
  spring water

2 tablespoons olive oil

1 cup Arborio or risotto rice

1 x 14 oz. can chopped
  tomatoes with herbs

1¾ cups hot stock

¾ cups fresh or frozen peas
  (no need to thaw if frozen)

salt and freshly ground
  black pepper

3 tablespoons freshly grated
  Parmesan cheese

a few fresh basil leaves,
  to garnish

*a medium-size heavy
  flameproof, ovenproof
  casserole with lid*

1 ASK AN ADULT TO HELP YOU preheat the oven to 350°F.

2 ASK AN ADULT TO HELP YOU trim the hairy ends off the scallions, then trim off the very dark green tops. Rinse the scallions in cold running water to get rid of any grit and mud. Using a small sharp knife, cut the scallions into thin rounds. Peel off the papery skins from the garlic, then crush or finely chop the cloves. Carefully open the cans of tuna and drain thoroughly in a colander.

3 Spoon the olive oil into the casserole. Set the casserole on the stove and ASK AN ADULT TO HELP YOU gently heat it. Using a wooden spoon, stir in the scallions and garlic and cook very gently for 1 minute.

4 Tip the rice into the casserole and stir well. Cook gently for 1 minute then stir in the contents of the can of tomatoes, followed by the stock and tuna. Stir well then add the peas and a little salt and black pepper. Stir once more then cover the casserole. ASK AN ADULT TO HELP YOU put the casserole in the preheated oven to bake for 35 minutes.

5 ASK AN ADULT TO HELP YOU remove the casserole from the oven. Before serving, remove the lid, then scatter over the Parmesan cheese and some gently torn basil leaves. Eat immediately. This is lovely with a salad made from green leaves and some cherry tomatoes.

Part of the fun of holidays is discovering new foods, and we've had some good crab cakes in Maine, as well as in San Francisco. These are like the ones from our favorite lobster shack on the beach, made with crunchy "oyster" crackers (the oyster-shaped, slightly salted plain crackers served with chowder), and served in a bun with coleslaw on the side. Here the ingredients are mixed together, shaped, then baked until golden and crispy. Just add a salad or fries!

oven-baked crunchy crab cakes

Serves 4

1 lb. white crabmeat (fresh, frozen, or canned)
about 12 cream crackers or 12 oz. oyster crackers
a small bunch of fresh parsley
1 extra-large egg
2 tablespoons good mayonnaise
½ a lemon
½ teaspoon dry mustard powder
½ teaspoon sweet paprika
a dash of Worcestershire sauce
a dash of Tabasco sauce (optional)
a little salt and freshly ground black pepper

a nonstick baking sheet, or large baking dish, greased

1 Drain the crabmeat or thaw it completely, then put it in a large mixing bowl.

2 Smash up the crackers: to do this, put them into a plastic bag and smash with a rolling pin to make fine crumbs. Measure out 5 tablespoons of the cracker crumbs and put these into the bowl with the crab. Save the rest of the crumbs for coating the crab cakes.

3 Rinse the parsley in cold running water and pat dry with paper towels. ASK AN ADULT TO HELP YOU chop up the parsley with a sharp knife (or with a herb chopper) and add to the crab. Using a table fork, gently mix the ingredients together.

4 Break the egg into a small bowl and pick out any pieces of shell, then add the mayonnaise. Squeeze the juice from the lemon half with a lemon squeezer. Pour into the bowl with the mayonnaise. Add the mustard, paprika, Worcestershire sauce, Tabasco (if using), and a little salt and pepper and mix together well with a fork.

5 Pour the egg mixture onto the crab mixture and mix thoroughly with a fork.

6 Divide the mixture into 8 equal portions. Using your hands, shape and press each portion into a ball, just like making a snowball, then pat out the ball to a cake about 3 inches across.

7 Put the rest of the cracker crumbs into a shallow dish. Gently dip each crab cake in the crumbs, and scatter some on top, so each cake is lightly coated in crumbs. Set the cakes on the prepared baking sheet or dish, slightly apart, then cover with plastic wrap and chill in the fridge for at least 2 hours and up to 6 hours.

8 When ready to cook, ASK AN ADULT TO HELP YOU preheat the oven to 400°F. Remove the plastic wrap from the crab cakes and ASK AN ADULT TO HELP YOU put them in the preheated oven to bake for 15 minutes, until golden and crispy. ASK AN ADULT TO HELP YOU remove the tray from the oven. Serve your crab cakes hot, with salad, warm rolls, and coleslaw.

Make your very own, healthy version of chicken nuggets. Strips of chicken breast are dipped in melted butter then coated in a savory crumb mixture and baked in the oven. Eat with Thai sweet chili dipping sauce rather than ketchup, and potato wedges, plus a salad.

oven-fried chicken nuggets with potato wedges

Serves 4

4 medium chicken breasts, skinless and boneless
4 tablespoons unsalted butter
2 cups fresh bread crumbs (see tip below)
1 teaspoon sweet paprika
¼ teaspoon dried mixed herbs or dried Italian herbs
a good pinch of salt
freshly ground black pepper

a large nonstick baking sheet or roasting pan, lightly oiled

Potato wedges:
4 medium baking potatoes
4 tablespoons olive oil
a little salt and freshly ground black pepper

a nonstick roasting pan

1 ASK AN ADULT TO HELP YOU preheat the oven to 400°F. Put the chicken breasts onto a cutting board. ASK AN ADULT TO HELP YOU slice each chicken breast into 5 strips diagonally, using a small sharp knife. Wash your hands then put the butter into a small saucepan and melt gently over low heat.

2 Carefully remove the pan from the heat and put onto a heatproof counter near the cutting board with the chicken strips.

3 Put the bread crumbs in a large, clean plastic bag. Add the paprika, dried herbs, salt, and pepper. Close the bag and shake well to mix.

4 Dip each strip of chicken into the melted butter then put it into the plastic bag with the crumbs. When all the chicken strips are in the bag, close it tightly and shake it well so the chicken gets coated in the crumbs.

5 Remove each chicken strip from the bag and put it on the prepared baking sheet, arranging the strips slightly apart and in one layer.

6 ASK AN ADULT TO HELP YOU put the strips in the preheated oven to bake for 15–20 minutes, until golden brown and nicely crisp. ASK AN ADULT TO HELP YOU remove the sheet from the oven. Use tongs or a fish slice to transfer the chicken to a serving platter and eat immediately.

Tip: To make your own bread crumbs, use sliced bread that is 1 or 2 days old. Carefully cut off the crusts, (you don't need them) then tear each slice of bread into about 8 pieces. ASK AN ADULT TO HELP YOU put them in a food processor or blender and process to make fine crumbs.

Potato wedges

1 ASK AN ADULT TO HELP YOU preheat the oven to 400°F. Wash the potatoes in cold running water, scrubbing lightly with a vegetable brush to get rid of any earth. Pat dry with paper towels.

2 Put the potatoes on a cutting board. ASK AN ADULT TO HELP YOU carefully cut each potato in half lengthwise, using a sharp knife. Cut each half into 3 long wedges.

3 Put the wedges into the roasting pan. Spoon over the oil, and sprinkle with salt and pepper. Using your hands, gently toss the wedges so they get coated in the oil. Put them skin-side down in the tin.

4 ASK AN ADULT TO HELP YOU put the wedges in the preheated oven to bake for about 1 hour, until brown. ASK AN ADULT TO HELP YOU remove the pan from the oven and transfer the wedges to a serving dish. Eat them while they are still hot.

My son Dan's grandparents introduced him to *confit de canard* one Easter in Paris. When he returned he wanted to know how it was made so we could enjoy it without making a trip to France. Luckily it's very simple. Confit is the French way of preserving meat by lightly salting it and then gently cooking it in plenty of fat. It is then kept in the fat (in the fridge these days) until ready to serve. The legs are then quickly cooked until very hot and crispy, and eaten with potatoes or with lentils or white beans and a green salad. Don't forget to wash your hands really well after you have been touching the duck legs.

dan's duck confit

Serves 4

4 duck legs
1 tablespoon sea salt or Kosher salt
½ teaspoon coarsely ground black pepper
3 sprigs of fresh thyme
2 bay leaves
12 oz. can goose fat or 12 oz. pack lard

a heavy flameproof, ovenproof casserole with a lid

1 You'll need a casserole with a lid that will take the legs in a single layer, even if they are squashed together.

2 Wipe the duck legs with paper towels and put in a large mixing bowl. Mix the salt and pepper and rub all over each leg, on the skin side and the underside, and in all the nooks and crannies. Cover the bowl with plastic wrap and put into the fridge for 2–3 hours.

3 Uncover the legs and wipe them, one at a time, with paper towels to remove as much of the salt as possible. As you finish each leg, put it into the casserole skin-side down. The legs should be in a single layer but can slightly overlap and it's fine to squash them together. Scatter the thyme sprigs and bay leaves on top.

4 ASK AN ADULT TO HELP YOU preheat the oven to 300°F.

5 Set the casserole on top of the stove and ASK AN ADULT TO HELP YOU turn on the heat to low. Leave the casserole to heat up gently and to melt some of the fat on the duck legs. After about 10 minutes there should be a puddle of fat around the legs; if not, cook for 5 minutes longer. Turn off the heat and spoon the goose fat or lard over the legs. Cover the casserole with the lid then ASK AN ADULT TO HELP YOU put the confit in the preheated oven to bake for 2 hours, without opening the oven door if possible.

6 ASK AN ADULT TO remove the casserole from the oven—it is full of hot fat so you must be very careful! Leave it to cool on a heatproof surface. When completely cold, transfer the casserole to the fridge and leave for at least 1 day and up to 4 days for the flavors to develop.

7 To eat the duck, take the casserole out of the fridge and leave it at room temperature for a few hours to soften the fat. Carefully remove the legs from the fat, scraping off as much fat as possible with a round-bladed table knife.

8 Put the legs skin-side down in a cold nonstick skillet. Put the pan over low to medium heat. The legs sometimes splutter and spit so ASK AN ADULT TO HELP YOU cook the confit gently for

about 10 minutes, until the skin is crispy and brown. Carefully turn the legs over and cook the other side for 5–7 minutes until lightly browned.

9 Eat the duck confit warm from the pan, or keep it warm in a low oven while, WITH ADULT HELP, you fry some sliced cooked potatoes in the fat in the pan. Save the fat left from the casserole to make another batch of confit or use it for roasting potatoes.

Lean minced lamb mixed with mild, aromatic Middle Eastern spices is pressed onto skewers and baked until browned then eaten with pita breads and a simple yogurt dip. Add a couple of simple salads like sliced tomato, and grated carrot mixed with a little fresh lemon juice, seasoning, and sesame seeds.

lamb koftas with pita pockets

Serves 4

1¼ lb. lean minced lamb
1 small red onion
2 teaspoons mild paprika
1½ teaspoons ground
    coriander
1½ teaspoons ground cumin
¼ teaspoon ground cinnamon
4 grinds of freshly ground
    black pepper
a good pinch of salt
a few sprigs of fresh parsley
    or cilantro

For the dip:
¾ cup plain yogurt
a good pinch of salt
freshly ground black pepper
a small bunch of chives
a few sprigs fresh parsley
    or cilantro
8 small or picnic-size pitas,
    to serve

16 wooden skewers
a baking sheet or roasting
    pan, lined with foil
    and oiled

1 ASK AN ADULT TO HELP YOU preheat the oven to 425°F. Soak the skewers in a bowl of water (this stops the wood from burning in the oven). Meanwhile, make up the meat mix.

2 Tip the minced lamb into a large mixing bowl. Peel the skin away from the onion and throw it away. Carefully grate the onion onto the lamb using the coarse or large-hole side of a grater.

3 Measure the spices—paprika, ground coriander, ground cumin, ground cinnamon, black pepper—and salt into the bowl. Using kitchen scissors, snip the parsley or cilantro sprigs into the bowl. Put your hands into the bowl and mix together all the ingredients, squeezing it between your fingers until it looks evenly mixed. (If you have plenty of time, you can now cover the bowl and chill it in the fridge for up to 5 hours before finishing the recipe.)

4 Divide the meat mixture into 16 even portions. Using your hands, mold each portion of meat around a skewer to make an egg or sausage shape about 4 inches long. Arrange the skewers on the prepared baking sheet. Wash your hands thoroughly.

5 ASK AN ADULT TO HELP YOU put the baking sheet in the preheated oven and bake the koftas for 15 minutes, until well-browned.

6 While the meat is cooking, make the dip by mixing the yogurt with the salt and pepper. Snip the chives and parsley or cilantro into small pieces with kitchen scissors and mix into the yogurt. Spoon into a serving bowl.

7 When the koftas are ready, ASK AN ADULT TO HELP YOU lift the sheet out of the oven. Transfer the skewers to a serving plate and serve with the yogurt dip and warm pitas.

For this recipe you need good meaty spareribs or king ribs. For a filling supper, cook some large baking potatoes in the oven at the same time as you cook the ribs. You could also roast some sweetcorn to complete the meal or make a big green salad.

sticky maple ribs with roast sweetcorn

Serves 4

1 medium red onion
3 tablespoons maple syrup
3 tablespoons soy sauce
3 tablespoons tomato ketchup
1½ tablespoons mild mustard
1½ tablespoons
    Worcestershire sauce
freshly ground black pepper
3 lb. spareribs

a large, nonstick roasting pan

Easy roast corn:
4 fresh corn-on-the-cobs
5 tablespoons unsalted butter
a little freshly ground black
    pepper

*an ovenproof dish, large
    enough to take the
    sweetcorn in a single layer*

1 ASK AN ADULT TO HELP YOU preheat the oven to 375°F.

2 Add a little oil to the roasting pan and rub it around the inside with a piece of paper towel.

3 Peel the skin away from the onion and throw it away. Grate the onion into a large mixing bowl using the coarse or large hole side of a grater.

4 Add the maple syrup, soy sauce, tomato ketchup, mustard, Worcestershire sauce, and 4 grinds of black pepper. Mix together well.

5 Add the ribs to the bowl one at a time and use a metal spoon to thoroughly cover the ribs with the sticky glaze. Carefully lift the ribs into the prepared pan. Wash your hands thoroughly before doing anything else.

6 ASK AN ADULT TO HELP YOU put the roasting pan in the preheated oven. Bake for 30 minutes then ASK AN ADULT TO HELP YOU remove the pan from the oven. Using kitchen tongs, carefully turn over the ribs so they brown evenly.

7 ASK AN ADULT TO HELP YOU put the pan back in the oven and bake for another 30 minutes.

8 The ribs should be a dark golden brown and crispy around the edges. ASK AN ADULT TO HELP YOU lift the pan out of the oven. Carefully transfer the ribs to a serving plate and eat!

Easy roast corn

1 ASK AN ADULT TO HELP YOU preheat the oven to 375°F.

2 If the corn still has its green leafy covering it must be "shucked"—pull off the leaves from the top pointy end, then pull off all the silky hairs.

3 ASK AN ADULT TO HELP YOU melt the butter: either put it in a small saucepan over the lowest possible heat, or microwave it in a bowl on medium for about 20 seconds.

4 Pour the butter into the baking dish, add a little black pepper, then put the corn into the dish and turn them so they are well coated in butter.

5 ASK AN ADULT TO HELP YOU put the dish in the preheated oven to bake for 30 minutes. ASK AN ADULT TO HELP YOU turn the corn over twice during this time—cooking tongs work best for this. Leave to cool slightly before eating.

desserts

baked alaska

Makes 1 large cake

For the sponge:
¾ cup plus 2 tablespoons
   all-purpose flour
1 teaspoon baking powder
½ cup plus 1 tablespoon
   superfine sugar
1 stick butter, very soft
½ teaspoon vanilla extract
2 extra-large eggs
1 tablespoon milk

To finish:
1 pint strawberry ice cream
4 egg whites
1 cup plus 2 tablespoons
   superfine sugar
1½ cups or 5 oz. raspberries
confectioners' sugar

a springform cake pan,
   8 inches diameter
greaseproof paper
a baking sheet

1 ASK AN ADULT TO HELP YOU preheat the oven to 350°F. Put a little soft butter on a piece of paper towel and rub it around the inside of the cake pan. Put the pan on the greaseproof paper and draw around it. Cut just inside the line to make a disk of paper. Fit this into the base of the pan. Put to one side.

2 Sift the flour and baking powder into a mixing bowl. Stir in the sugar. Add the very soft butter and vanilla extract to the bowl.

3 Break the eggs into a small bowl. Pick out any pieces of shell then lightly beat the eggs and the milk with a fork to break them up. Pour the eggs into the mixing bowl. Beat all the ingredients with a wooden spoon, or ASK AN ADULT TO HELP YOU use an electric mixer or whisk, until the mixture is very smooth and light. Spoon the mixture into the prepared cake pan and spread it evenly around the pan.

4 ASK AN ADULT TO HELP YOU put the sponge cake in the preheated oven to bake for about 25 minutes, until a light golden brown. To test if the cake is cooked, ASK AN ADULT TO HELP YOU remove it from the oven and gently press it in the middle. If it springs back it is cooked; if there is a dimple then bake for 5 minutes more. ASK AN ADULT TO HELP YOU remove the sponge from the oven, leave for 2 minutes, then run a round-bladed knife around the inside of the pan and carefully turn out the cake onto a wire rack. Leave to cool completely. Turn off the oven.

5 Remove the ice cream from the freezer and leave until soft enough to spoon onto the sponge; put the sponge cake onto a baking sheet, then scoop or spoon the ice cream on top to make an even layer. Put the whole thing back into the freezer and leave until very firm—at least 1 hour, but you can leave it in the freezer for up to 3 days.

This is great fun to make and eat! You can use a ready-made sponge flan case or cake for the base, and choose your favorite flavor of ice cream. It's good served with a sauce made from ripe strawberries mashed using a fork or a blender, mixed with a little bit of confectioners' sugar.

6 When you are ready to finish the alaska, ASK AN ADULT TO HELP YOU preheat the oven to 425°F. Put the egg whites into a very clean mixing bowl. Stand the bowl on a damp cloth to keep it from wobbling. Using an electric mixer or hand whisk, beat until the whites turn into a stiff white foam— lift out the whisk and there will be a little peak of white standing on the end.

7 Quickly whisk the superfine sugar into the egg whites to make a stiff and glossy meringue.

8 Remove the sponge and ice cream from the freezer. Arrange the raspberries on top of the ice cream. Quickly cover the whole thing with the meringue, spreading it evenly. Make sure that there are no holes or gaps and the meringue covers every inch of the cake and ice cream. Sprinkle with sifted confectioners' sugar.

9 ASK AN ADULT TO HELP YOU put the alaska in the preheated oven to bake for just 4–5 minutes, until lightly browned. Serve immediately.

At first glance this fun dessert looks like a nutty meringue, but hidden underneath is an apple stuffed with apricots! Eat it with a scoop of vanilla ice cream.

apple hedgehogs

Makes 4 hedgehogs

4 small to medium very tart apples

8 ready-to-eat dried apricots

3 egg whites

¾ cup superfine or granulated sugar

4 tablespoons sliced or slivered almonds

a large shallow ovenproof baking dish

1 ASK AN ADULT TO HELP YOU preheat the oven to 350°F. Put a small amount of soft butter on a piece of paper towel and rub it around the inside of the baking dish.

2 Peel the apples with a vegetable peeler then remove the core with an apple corer—ASK AN ADULT TO HELP YOU if this is hard work.

3 Cut the apricots into small pieces with kitchen scissors. Set an apple in each baking dish or arrange them well apart in the large dish. Push the chopped-up apricots into the center hole in each apple.

4 Put the egg whites into a very clean and dry mixing bowl, or the bowl of an electric mixer. Use a wire whisk or the whisk attachment of the electric mixer to whisk the egg whites until they are very stiff, and the whisk leaves the mixture in very stiff pointy peaks when you lift it out.

5 Tip in the sugar and whisk again just until all the sugar has been combined. Spoon a quarter of the mixture on top of each apple, then spread the meringue mixture all over the apple to completely cover it. It should look quite rough. Stick the almonds into the meringue to look like the spines on a hedgehog.

6 ASK AN ADULT TO HELP YOU put the apples in the preheated oven to bake for 35 minutes, until a good golden brown.

7 ASK AN ADULT TO HELP YOU carefully remove the apple hedgehogs from the oven then leave them to cool for about 15 minutes before serving.

This is a light, baked cheesecake with lots of fresh raspberries, strawberries, and blueberries so it makes a lovely summer dessert. Ricotta is a low-fat soft Italian cheese usually sold in tubs.

lemon ricotta cheesecake with summer berries

Makes 1 large cheesecake

For the crust:
4 tablespoons unsalted butter
4½ oz. plain wheaten crackers or cookies
1 tablespoon superfine or granulated sugar

For the filling:
1 lb. tub ricotta cheese (about 2 cups)
1 cup sour cream
2 extra-large eggs
¾ cup confectioners' sugar
2 tablespoons sliced almonds, ground
2 medium unwaxed lemons

For the topping:
2 tablespoons slivered almonds
fresh summer berries, to serve

a springform cake pan or deep tart pan, 9 inch diameter

1 ASK AN ADULT TO HELP YOU preheat the oven to 300°F.

2 Lightly rub the inside of the pan with a little soft butter on a piece of paper towel.

3 ASK AN ADULT TO HELP YOU melt the butter for the crust: put the butter in a small saucepan and melt on the stove over low heat, or if you like, you can melt the butter in the microwave.

4 Put the crackers in a plastic bag. Make sure the ends of the bag are tightly closed then crush the crackers into crumbs by hitting them with a rolling pin. Tip the crumbs into a mixing bowl and add the melted butter and the superfine sugar. Mix well with a wooden spoon then tip the mixture into the pan.

5 Roughly spread the crumbs in the pan so they are evenly distributed then, using the back of a metal spoon, press the crumbs onto the base of the pan to make an even layer. Put the pan in the fridge to chill while you make the filling.

6 Put the ricotta and sour cream into a large mixing bowl or the bowl of a food processor. Break the eggs into the bowl, remove any pieces of shell, then add the confectioners' sugar and ground almonds.

7 Rinse the lemons then grate the yellow zest straight into the bowl using a lemon zester or a fine grater. Cut the lemons in half and squeeze out the juice with a lemon squeezer. Pour the juice into the bowl.

8 Mix all the ingredients together using a wooden spoon until completely smooth. ASK AN ADULT TO HELP YOU blend the ingredients in a food processor or if you want to use an electric mixer (use slow speed).

9 Pour the filling carefully into the pan then scatter the flaked almonds on the top.

10 ASK AN ADULT TO HELP YOU put the pan in the preheated oven. Bake for 1¼ hours then turn off the oven and leave the cheesecake inside (don't open the door) to cool slowly as the oven cools down. After 1½ hours, remove it from the oven. If you have used a springform pan, gently remove the cheesecake from the pan.

11 Store your cheesecake in an airtight container in the fridge and eat it within 3 days. For the best flavor, remove it from the fridge about 30 minutes before eating. Serve the cheesecake either topped with or surrounded by the berries or put them in a separate bowl so everyone can help themselves.

chocolate & coconut rice pudding

Serves 4–6

¼ cup slightly heaped Arborio
   or risotto rice
3 tablespoons superfine or
   granulated sugar
14 oz. can coconut milk or
   1¾ cups whole milk
2 cups milk
2 oz. bittersweet chocolate

an ovenproof baking dish,
   about 2 pints capacity,
   buttered

1 ASK AN ADULT TO HELP YOU preheat the oven to 300°F.

2 Put the rice and sugar in the prepared baking dish. Pour the coconut milk and milk into the dish and stir gently.

3 ASK AN ADULT TO HELP YOU put the pudding in the preheated oven to bake for 2 hours, then WITH ADULT HELP carefully take the pudding out of the oven. Stir it very gently with a wooden spoon to break up the skin and mix well.

4 Break up the chocolate and scatter the pieces over the pudding. Stir just to marble the chocolate through the pudding.

5 ASK AN ADULT TO HELP YOU put the pudding back in the oven and bake it for another 30 minutes. WITH ADULT HELP, carefully remove the pudding from the oven and let it cool for 20–30 minutes before eating.

Coconut and toffee pudding: make the pudding as above and bake it for 2 hours. ASK AN ADULT TO HELP YOU remove it from the oven but do not stir. Sprinkle ⅓ cup firm-packed soft dark brown sugar or molasses sugar (instead of chocolate) over the surface. Return to the oven and bake for a further 30 minutes. WITH ADULT HELP, remove it from the oven and let it cool for 30 minutes before serving.

An easy-to-make rice pudding that's good eaten warm or at room temperature. If you don't like the taste of coconut, you can use extra ordinary milk instead.

This is a lovely fruity tart that's just right for eating after a big Sunday lunch as it's not too filling. Serve it with custard or ice cream.

lemon & apple tart

Makes 1 large pie

12 oz. shortcrust dough
   (see note below)
2–3 or about 10 oz. very tart
   apples
3 rounded tablespoons golden
   syrup or dark corn syrup
2 oz. or about 2 slices
   crustless bread
1 large unwaxed lemon

*a shallow pie plate or tart
   pan, 10 inches diameter*

1 ASK AN ADULT TO HELP YOU preheat the oven to 375°F. Sprinkle a little flour on your work surface, then gently roll out the dough (using a rolling pin sprinkled with flour) to a circle the same size as your pie plate. Roll the dough round the rolling pin then lift it over the plate so the dough drapes over it. Carefully press the dough onto the base, making sure you have pressed out any pockets of air. Finally, press the dough onto the rim.

2 With kitchen scissors, carefully snip off any excess dough that is hanging over the edge of the plate (you can save this to make some decorations). Decorate the rim of the tart by pressing the dough with the prongs of a fork to make a stripey pattern. Put the pie plate in the fridge to chill while you make the filling.

3 Peel the apples with a vegetable peeler, then remove the core with an apple corer or ASK AN ADULT TO HELP YOU cut the apple into quarters, then cut out the core. Grate the apple into a mixing bowl. Add the golden syrup to the bowl.

4 Break up the bread and put it in a food processor or blender. ASK AN ADULT TO HELP YOU process it to make fine crumbs. Tip the crumbs into the bowl with the apple. Rinse the lemon in cold running water and pat dry. Grate the yellow zest straight into the mixing bowl

using a lemon zester or fine grater. Cut the lemon in half and squeeze out the juice with a lemon squeezer. Pour the juice into the bowl with the other ingredients.

5 Mix all the ingredients really well using a table fork in each hand to stir everything together. Gently spoon the filling onto the dough base— don't press the filling or it might lose its fluffy texture. You can decorate the tart with dough scraps cut into shapes using fancy cutters or dough strips to make a lattice pattern on top.

6 ASK AN ADULT TO HELP YOU put the tart in the preheated oven to bake for 30 minutes, until golden. ASK AN ADULT TO HELP YOU remove it from the oven and eat warm or at room temperature with yogurt or ice cream. Your tart is best eaten within 2 days of baking.

Shortcrust pastry: you can use ready-made fresh or frozen dough (defrost according to the package instructions). Some brands make sheets of ready-rolled pastry. To make your own, put 1½ cups all-purpose flour and a pinch of salt into the bowl of a food processor. Add 1½ sticks unsalted butter (straight from the fridge), cut into small pieces. ASK AN ADULT TO HELP YOU process it until the mixture makes fine crumbs. Add 2 tablespoons of icy cold water and process again until the dough comes together in a ball.

The appeal of this fruit tart is its rustic, homemade charm. This is nothing like a tart from a fancy patisserie! Use slightly underripe peaches, pears, or dessert apples, and you can add nuts, raisins, or sultanas and a little cinnamon when you mix in the sugar.

free-form peach pie

1 First make the dough using the food processor: put the flour, salt, cinnamon, and sugar into the bowl of the processor. ASK AN ADULT TO HELP YOU run the machine for a few seconds just to combine all the ingredients.

2 Cut the butter into small pieces and add to the bowl of the processor and ASK AN ADULT TO HELP YOU run the machine until the ingredients look like coarse crumbs. Pour in the water through the feed tube and run the machine until the dough comes together in a ball.

3 Sprinkle a little flour on your kitchen counter. WITH ADULT HELP, carefully remove the dough from the processor. Put the dough onto the counter and gently knead and work the dough for a few seconds until the dough looks smooth.

4 Put the sheet of nonstick baking parchment onto the work surface. Put the ball of dough in the middle of the paper. Sprinkle a rolling pin with flour and gently roll out the dough to a circle about 12 inches across. Slide the sheet of paper with the dough on it onto the baking sheet and chill in the fridge for 15 minutes while you make the filling.

5 ASK AN ADULT TO HELP YOU preheat the oven to 400°F. Rinse the fruit in cold running water and pat dry. WITH ADULT HELP, slice the peaches in half along the line that runs from the stem

down to the base. Twist the peach so the two halves separate. Pull the halves apart and remove the stone. Cut each half into 4 thick slices. If using apples, peel them only if the skin is tough. Quarter them, cut out the cores, and slice thickly. Peel the pears with a potato peeler, quarter them, cut out the cores, and slice thickly.

6 Sprinkle the sliced fruit with the 3 tablespoons sugar, and mix gently. Remove the dough from the fridge. Heap the sliced fruit into the center of the dough, mounding it evenly. Leave a wide border of dough, about 3 inches, without fruit.

7 Gently fold the border of dough over the fruit so the fruit in the center is uncovered, leaving a gap of about 1 inch between the fruit and the fold, and gently pinch the folds or pleats of dough together every 3 inches. Try not to press the dough down onto the fruit.

8 Using a pastry brush, lightly brush the dough with cold water then sprinkle with superfine sugar.

9 ASK AN ADULT TO HELP YOU put the pie in the preheated oven to bake for 40 minutes, until golden brown. ASK AN ADULT TO HELP YOU remove it from the oven and leave to cool on its tray for 10 minutes. Slide the tart off its paper lining and onto a serving platter while it is still warm, and serve.

Makes 1 large pie

For the pastry:
1⅔ cup all-purpose flour
a good pinch of salt
a good pinch of ground
   cinnamon
2 tablespoons superfine or
   granulated sugar
5½ oz. unsalted butter,
   straight from the fridge
3 tablespoons cold water

For the filling:
5 medium peaches, about
   1½ lb., eating apples
   or pears
3 tablespoons superfine or
   granulated sugar, plus extra
   for sprinkling

a large baking sheet
a sheet of nonstick baking
   parchment

Another family holiday favorite, this time from France. A clafoutis is a dessert made from fresh cherries baked in a rich custardy topping. I've added blueberries and blackberries to my own recipe, but you can also use pears (peeled, cored, and diced) or sliced fresh apricots.

cherry & berry clafoutis

Makes 1 large clafoutis

½ **cup blueberries**

½ **cup blackberries or black raspberries**

7 oz. cherries

2 very large eggs

1 cup crème fraiche or heavy cream

½ **cup superfine or granulated sugar, plus extra for sprinkling**

2 tablespoons all-purpose flour

½ **teaspoon vanilla extract**

a shallow ovenproof dish about 3 pints capacity, greased

1 ASK AN ADULT TO HELP YOU preheat the oven to 350°F.

2 Rinse the blueberries and blackberries in a colander in cold running water. Drain thoroughly then put them in the prepared baking dish.

3 Rinse the cherries then ASK AN ADULT TO HELP YOU remove the stones with a cherry stoner. Put them on top of the berries.

4 Break the eggs into a mixing bowl and pick out any pieces of shell. Add the crème fraiche or cream, sugar, flour, and vanilla extract to the mixing bowl. Beat gently with a wire whisk or fork until thoroughly mixed.

5 Carefully pour the egg mixture over the fruit. Sprinkle with a little extra sugar then ASK AN ADULT TO HELP YOU put the clafoutis into the preheated oven to bake for about 35 minutes, until golden and just set when you gently wobble the dish.

6 ASK AN ADULT TO HELP YOU remove the dish from the oven, leave it for 15 minutes on a heatproof counter and then eat it while it is still warm with a scoop of vanilla ice cream.

On holiday in Vermont we visited a bakery and this maple pie was a big hit! Early each spring the maple trees there are tapped to produce the sap, which is boiled down to make syrup. It takes 40 gallons of sap to make just one gallon of the wonderful syrup!

maple pie

Makes 1 large pie

For the pastry:
2½ cups all-purpose flour
a pinch of salt
1¾ sticks unsalted butter,
   straight from the fridge
3 tablespoons icy-cold water
or
1 lb. ready-made pastry
   dough, defrosted if
   necessary

For the filling:
2 extra-large eggs
1¼ cups maple syrup
⅔ cup heavy cream
2 tablespoons all-purpose
   flour
1 cup walnut pieces
confectioners' sugar or maple
   sugar, for sprinkling

a deep pie dish or tart pan,
*   9 inches diameter*
a baking sheet
nonstick baking parchment
shaped cookie cutters

1 First make the pastry dough, unless you are using the ready-made pastry dough. Put the flour and salt into the bowl of a food processor. Cut the butter into small chunks and add to the bowl. ASK AN ADULT TO HELP YOU run the machine until the mixture looks like fine crumbs. Pour in the cold water through the feed tube and run the machine until the crumbs come together to make a firm dough. ASK AN ADULT TO HELP YOU remove the dough from the bowl.

2 Scatter a little flour over the work surface. Put the dough or ready-made pastry dough on the floured surface and gently roll out with a rolling pin to a large circle 14 inches across. Roll the circle around the rolling pin and lift it over the pie dish. Gently unroll the dough so it drapes over the dish. Carefully press the dough onto the bottom of the dish and up the sides so there are no bubbles of air. Roll the pin over the top of the dish to cut off the overhanging dough (or snip it off with kitchen scissors). Save the dough for the decorations. Gently use your thumbs to press the dough sides up so the pastry stands about 2 inches higher than the rim of the dish. Prick the base a few times with a fork, then chill in the fridge for 20 minutes.

3 ASK AN ADULT TO HELP YOU preheat the oven to 400°F. Take the chilled pastry in its pie dish out of the fridge. Cut a round of nonstick baking parchment 14 inches across. Crumple the paper to make it soft then open it out and gently press it into the pastry case to cover the base and sides. Fill the case with baking beans, dried beans, or uncooked rice to weigh the paper down. ASK AN ADULT TO HELP YOU put it in the preheated oven to bake for 15 minutes. ASK AN ADULT TO HELP YOU remove the pastry shell from the oven and carefully remove the paper and beans. Turn the oven down to 375°F and bake the pastry case for 5 minutes more, until a light gold color. Put a baking sheet into the oven to heat up.

4 To make the filling, break the eggs into a mixing bowl or large jug. Pick out any pieces of shell. Add the maple syrup, cream, and flour and mix well with a wire whisk until smooth.

5 ASK AN ADULT TO HELP YOU remove the pastry shell from the oven. Stand the pastry shell in its pie dish on the hot baking sheet. Scatter the walnuts over the base of the pastry shell. Carefully pour the filling over the nuts then ASK AN ADULT TO HELP YOU put it in the oven to bake for 30 minutes, until lightly colored.

6 Roll out the leftover dough fairly thinly and cut into shapes using fancy cookie cutters (maple leaves or whatever you like). ASK AN ADULT TO HELP YOU remove the pie from the oven and gently arrange the pastry shapes on top. Return the pie to the oven and bake for 10 minutes more. WITH ADULT HELP, carefully remove it from the oven and leave to cool. Eat while still warm. Sprinkle with confectioners' sugar or maple sugar before serving.

These are rich but light puddings, made without flour. If you don't want to use nuts, you can replace the ground almonds with 2 tablespoons of all-purpose flour. Eat warm from the oven, topped with a scoop of vanilla or white chocolate ice cream. Yum!

warm chocolate puddings

Makes 6 small puddings

5½ oz. bittersweet chocolate

7 tablespoons unsalted butter

2 extra large eggs, at room temperature

2 egg yolks, at room temperature

5 tablespoons superfine or granulated sugar

2 tablespoons sliced almonds, ground

6 x ²⁄₃-cup ramekins or similar ovenproof dishes

a baking sheet

1 ASK AN ADULT TO HELP YOU preheat the oven to 425°F. Put a little soft butter on a piece of paper towel and rub inside the ramekins, then set the ramekins on a baking sheet.

2 Break up the chocolate and put it in a heatproof mixing bowl. Cut up the butter into chunks and add to the bowl.

3 Half fill a medium saucepan with water and WITH ADULT HELP put it on the stove and heat until the water boils. Turn off the heat and carefully set the mixing bowl containing the chocolate and butter over the hot water and leave to melt gently.

4 While the chocolate melts, put the 2 whole eggs, the 2 egg yolks, and sugar into a mixing bowl or the bowl of an electric mixer. Using a wire whisk or electric whisk or mixer beat the mixture until very light and foamy. Add the ground almonds and whisk for a few seconds.

5 Gently stir the chocolate mixture until smooth. ASK AN ADULT TO HELP YOU remove the bowl from the pan of hot water. Pour the chocolate mixture onto the egg mixture, scrape out the bowl, then whisk until the two mixtures are thoroughly blended.

6 Carefully spoon the chocolate mixture into the prepared ramekins so there is the same amount in each. ASK AN ADULT TO HELP YOU put the baking sheet with the ramekins on in the preheated oven to bake for 10 minutes, until slightly puffed and just soft in the middle. ASK AN ADULT TO HELP YOU carefully remove them from the oven and serve them immediately with a scoop of ice cream on top of each pudding.

sticky toffee pudding

Makes 1 large pudding

For the pudding:
1 cup stoned chopped dates
1¼ cups boiling water
1 teaspoon bicarbonate
 of soda
4 tablespoons unsalted butter,
 very soft
¾ cup superfine or
 granulated sugar
½ teaspoon vanilla extract
2 extra-large eggs, at room
 temperature
1⅔ cups all-purpose flour
1 teaspoon baking powder

For the sauce:
⅔ cup firm-packed soft dark
 brown sugar
4 tablespoons unsalted butter
1 cup light cream

an ovenproof baking dish,
 about 3 pints capacity,
 greased

1 ASK AN ADULT TO HELP YOU preheat the oven to 350°F.

2 Put the dates in a small saucepan or heatproof bowl. ASK AN ADULT TO HELP YOU pour over the boiling water then stir in the bicarbonate of soda and leave to soak until needed.

3 Put the butter in a mixing bowl or the bowl of an electric mixer. Add the superfine sugar and the vanilla extract and beat with a wooden spoon or electric whisk (WITH ADULT HELP) until very well combined (the mixture won't look soft and fluffy like a sponge cake mix).

4 Break the eggs into a bowl or small jug, pick out any pieces of shell, then beat with a fork just to break up the eggs. Pour a little of the egg mix into the mixing bowl and beat well. Keep on adding the eggs, a little at a time, then beating well, until all the eggs have been used up.

5 Set a strainer over the bowl and tip the flour and baking powder into the strainer and sift into the bowl. Stir gently a few times to half-mix in the flour, then pour the date and water mixture into the bowl. Carefully mix the whole lot together to make a runny batter.

6 Pour the pudding batter into the prepared dish. ASK AN ADULT TO HELP YOU put the pudding in the preheated oven to bake for about 40–45 minutes, until golden brown. To test if the pudding is cooked, ASK AN ADULT TO HELP YOU remove it from the oven and push a toothpick into the center. If the stick comes out clean then the pudding is cooked; if the stick is sticky with mixture then the pudding needs another 5 minutes in the oven, before you test it again.

7 While the pudding is baking, make the sauce. Put the brown sugar, butter, and cream into a small saucepan. ASK AN ADULT TO HELP YOU set the pan over low heat and heat gently, stirring now and then until melted, smooth, and hot.

8 ASK AN ADULT TO HELP YOU remove the pudding from the oven. Serve it warm with the hot sauce. Any leftover pudding and sauce can be gently reheated and served again. Eat within 2 days of making.

A really popular sticky pudding from the Lake District of northern England that is just perfect for a cold day. The toffee sauce is also good with ice cream.

index

conversion charts

Weights and measures have been rounded up or down slightly to make measuring easier.

Measuring butter:
A US stick of butter weighs 4 oz. which is approximately 115 g or 8 tablespoons. The recipes in this book require the following conversions:

American	Metric	Imperial
6 tbsp	85 g	3 oz.
7 tbsp	100 g	3½ oz.
1 stick	115 g	4 oz.

Volume equivalents:

American	Metric	Imperial
1 teaspoon	5 ml	
1 tablespoon	15 ml	
¼ cup	60 ml	2 fl.oz.
⅓ cup	75 ml	2½ fl.oz.
½ cup	125 ml	4 fl.oz.
⅔ cup	150 ml	5 fl.oz. (¼ pint)
¾ cup	175 ml	6 fl.oz.
1 cup	250 ml	8 fl.oz.

Weight equivalents:

Imperial	Metric
1 oz.	30 g
2 oz.	55 g
3 oz.	85 g
3½ oz.	100 g
4 oz.	115 g
5 oz.	140 g
6 oz.	175 g
8 oz. (½ lb.)	225 g
9 oz.	250 g
10 oz.	280 g
11½ oz.	325 g
12 oz.	350 g
13 oz.	375 g
14 oz.	400 g
15 oz.	425 g
16 oz. (1 lb.)	450 g

Measurements:

Inches	Cm
¼ inch	5 mm
½ inch	1 cm
¾ inch	1.5 cm
1 inch	2.5 cm
2 inches	5 cm
3 inches	7 cm
4 inches	10 cm
5 inches	12 cm
6 inches	15 cm
7 inches	18 cm
8 inches	20 cm
9 inches	23 cm
10 inches	25 cm
11 inches	28 cm
12 inches	30 cm

Oven temperatures:

150°C	(300°F)	Gas 2
170°C	(325°F)	Gas 3
180°C	(350°F)	Gas 4
190°C	(375°F)	Gas 5
200°C	(400°F)	Gas 6

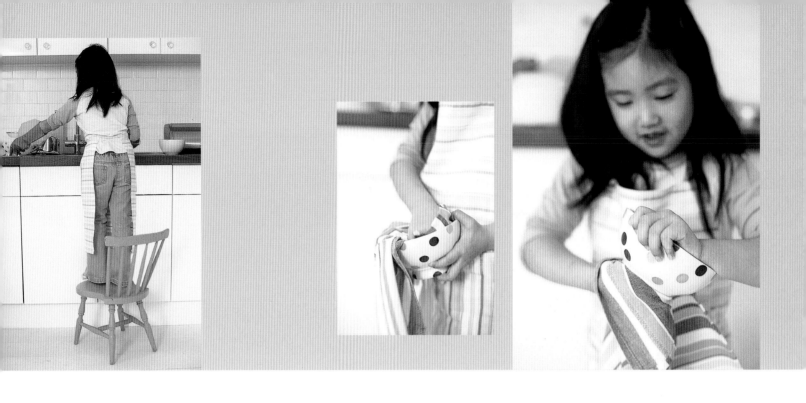

acknowledgments

The publishers would like to say thank you to all our lovely models, especially Ruby and Savannah, Seren, Max, Phoebe and Yasmin, Davian and Jerrell, Maria, Tabitha, Charlie, Beau and Jake, as well as Molly.

Very special thanks also to Gail Taylor, Amanda Trent, Fiona Sullivan, Kerri Goulty, Elizabeth James, and Sandy of Pregnant Pause Agency.

The publishers would also like to thank Jacqs at Millie Mac for supplying the aprons and oven gloves on the following pages: 2, 6, 9, 16, 17, 22, 23, and 77.

Millie Mac
5 Sunnyside Road
Teddington
Middlesex TW11 0RP
UK
www.milliemac.co.uk
tel: + 44 (0)20 8977 5779
*High-quality and handmade range of
children's and adults products from
oven gloves and aprons to bags and bibs.*